D1473881

making teen parties click

Stackpole Books Harrisburg, Pennsylvania

making teen parties click

Mary K. Robb

Illustrations by Bob Roumfort

Library of Congress catalog card number: 65-21623
Printed in the U.S.A. by The Telegraph Press, Harrisburg, Pa.

10

To
Ted and
the Many Friends
Who Attended
Our
Parties

Preface

When youth leaders, teachers, church workers, and parents are faced with planning social or recreational programs for teen-agers, they are often perplexed. Not only do they wonder what activities they can plan so that everyone will have an enjoyable time; they are also concerned with how to motivate teen-agers so they all will take part in the fun.

If you are planning a teen-age program, don't let the thought of giving a party get you down. Just visualize a group of fun-loving, congenial, happy teen-agers all laughing, chatting, dancing, playing together, and having a wonderful time.

Dozens of questions will pop into your mind. What can I do to get things going when I have a party? Will the boys stand on one side of the room and the girls huddle together on the other? What will I do if the guests just sit? How can I avoid a circle of half-quiet guests? (This is a situation in which a clock can be heard ticking but the hands seem to be standing still!) Good program planning can preclude such calamities.

This book will help you plan a teen-age party for any occasion, at home or away, from beginning to end. The activities and hints for leadership are stated in simple language. The programs are based entirely upon group participation. They are arranged so that all the teen-agers will enter into the fun with enthusiasm.

I have worked with teen-age groups for many years. Needless to say, then, my search for suitable material has been constant. So often after a party, the teen-agers will say: "We had such a wonderful time. We hope we can have another party like this real soon." Remarks like these have inspired me to share my experiences and pass along to parents and youth leaders the knowledge I have gained about the mannerisms of teen-agers and the games and activities my youth groups have enjoyed so enthusiastically.

After a well-planned party, your teen-agers will go home cherishing the memories of an enjoyable evening. What more can be said of a party than that *everyone had fun?*

Here's to the wonderful, fun-packed teen-age parties you can plan from the suggestions given in this book.

Acknowledgments

Numerous friends deserve sincere thanks and appreciation for their inspiration, helpful consultations, and other assistance in publishing this book. I wish especially to thank Marilynn Burdick Stadtmiller for her help and Robert Roumfort for his artistic contributions.

Appreciation is expressed to the parents and teen-agers on Auburn Street, without whose help and assistance I would not have been able to test and incorporate many of my party ideas.

I also wish to thank, for their zest and fun-loving spirits, the thousands of teen-agers with whom it has been my privilege and pleasure to work on many festive occasions.

Contents

1 about teen-agers

Adults are adults, and teen-agers are teen-agers—the difference is just a matter of years. Therefore it is necessary that parents and those who work with teen-age groups know something about their physical, mental, social, and emotional growth. Teen-agers attending social functions are boys and girls who are growing up and learning to adjust to an almost new world.

Teen-agers mature at different rates of speed. Girls usually mature earlier than boys. Planning parties and activities for teen-agers would be easier if the groups were separated in terms of their maturity level rather than their chronological age. Because of the different levels of maturity, it takes considerable understanding and skill on the part of parents, youth leaders, and recreation directors to plan parties and recreational programs that will interest and satisfy those who are still young as well as those who are more advanced in their physical development.

the young teens

By the time the boys and girls have reached their thirteenth year, birthday parties have almost lost their glamour. Girls at this age become interested in boy-girl parties. A boy's biggest interest in going to a party at this age, however, is usually to eat, tease and trip the girls, or throw things at them. The interests of boys and girls at this period are definitely not on the same level. Boys like "rough and ready" games, but girls usually prefer more subdued activities. Through motivation they will mix in school and planned parties, but in unguided activities the boys prefer to share activities with boys.

the middle teens

Fifteen-year-old girls are much more mature than the boys at this age. Girls become interested in dates and dancing long before the boys with whom they are associated begin even to think of such things. When these girls attend social functions, they often find that boys are not very attentive party companions. If the leader announces "girl's choice," the young teen-age girl may look around to see her special "boyfriend" going off in the opposite direction. Girls often leave these parties unhappy, with a feeling of social failure, because the boys did not seem to show any interest in them. Ten chances to one this had nothing to do with appearance or personality. Boys at this age are frequently shy or wrapped up in masculine things—baseball, basketball, combos, racing cars, and the like—and just are not interested in "wasting time" with girls. Boys would rather stand around and have spontaneous fun like turning out lights or shoving each other around. The following letter, presented here by permission of Ann Landers, expresses well the dilemma of teen-age girls when they attend parties with boys of this age:

Dear Ann Landers:

I am a girl of fifteen. Whoever started that big story that teen-age years are the happiest in a person's life must have been out of his head.

I want to direct this letter to teen-age boys because they are the main reason for the misery of many, many teen-age girls.

At every party—whether it's a school hop, at somebody's house, or a church get-together—you will always see a group of girls standing in a circle. They are laughing and talking, and at a glance you think they are having a wonderful time.

The truth is they are having a lousy time and they wish they had stayed home. These girls stick together and try to look gay because no boy will ask them to dance. All the boys run after the two or three pretty and popular girls. The plainer ones, like me, never get asked for a single dance. It's humiliating and heartbreaking. This letter is a plea to teen-age boys to be more thoughtful and considerate. So what if a girl is not a great dancer or a living doll? She may have lots more on the ball than the others if you give her a chance to show it. One thing is certain, she'll appreciate you a lot more than the girl who is run ragged by every fellow in the place.

The next time you go to a party or dance, seek that circle of girls who stick together because misery loves company. Get another fellow or two to join you, and ask the wall flowers to dance or accompany you to the refreshment table. You'll be doing a marvelous thing for two people—the girl and yourself.

(signed) Bitter Fifteen

Dear Bitter Fifteen:

What is there for me to say? You've said it all.

ANN LANDERS

Some girls who do not understand the difference in development between boys and girls try to overcome their frustrations by bleaching or overdressing their hair, using too much lipstick, wearing skirts too tight or too short, or "chasing" after boys in an effort to attract them. Boys at this age who are girl-shy and busy with other things need a friendly push, but running after a boy is very different from asking him to a party.

By the time teen-agers reach their sixteenth year, a few of the boys start to dance voluntarily with the girls at a party. The fellows do not stand and "horse around" so much—except for the few who are afraid to ask a girl to dance because they might be refused. Some may also fear that if an invitation is accepted, they will not be able to dance well enough to please the girls. These boys stand around together making their own fun.

the older teens

At later teen-age parties, many of the guests will arrive in couples, because they are "going steady." This means that they will dance with the same person all evening and pay little attention to anyone else. Other guests will not be "going steady," but by pre-arrangement a number of boys will meet girls at the dance. Some girls will arrive with a group of girls and hope the boys will ask to take them home. The fellows who arrive together are not particularly interested in dancing, but they are mildly interested in the girls. A girl at this kind of party may have more opportunities to dance than she has had at similar parties for younger age groups.

As teen-age boys advance to the maturity level of girls and begin to feel a genuine interest, teen-age parties and social functions become more settled and the atmosphere is calmer.

At still older teen-age parties, the task of getting the boys to dance with the girls is of little consequence. It's no longer a problem. By now conversation comes more easily, interests are more on the same level, many social graces have been acquired, and the teen-agers are at ease in each other's company. Couples might wander away from the group, but they usually return in a short time. Correction of the immature boys is still necessary, and uninvited guests or boys who have been drinking may have to be barred from the party.

Parents and youth leaders encounter "trouble spots" of different types at each level. One must be understanding and sensitive to the moods of the teen-agers and must have the ability to discipline them when necessary. You can win their respect by being open-minded and by making harmonious plans to meet the desires of a group of teen-agers who are thinking and acting on different levels. This is not an easy task. It takes perseverance and patience.

emotional factors in teen-age behavior

The keynote of success with teen-age groups is not in training or in the quantity of ideas, but rather in willingness to seek, understand, and establish a co-operative relationship with the teen-ager. When a group of teen-agers seems noisy, inconsiderate, and difficult to work with, there are usually some underlying motives at work.

Psychologists tell us that one of man's basic needs is to possess the feeling of belonging. Being liked and accepted by others is vital to a teen-ager. He needs to feel wanted and appreciated, and his awareness of this need makes a difference in the way a teen-ager responds to a suggestion or situation. Adults who care must make active and continuous efforts to create within each teen-ager a feeling of belonging. They need to offer help and guidance to the unfortunate ones who suffer heartaches and frustrations because they are not accepted by the group.

Sometimes an insecure teen-ager will rebel against others and assert himself in unbecoming ways, to prove to himself that he is right. He may assume a "big shot" attitude—talk with a loud voice, criticize the way everything is going, and refuse to co-operate. Or he might call the attention of the group to his presence by deliberately falling from his chair or doing any number of smart aleck things.

Regardless of his maturity level or chronological age, a teen-ager wants to feel some degree of importance. He neither wants to be told what to do nor wishes to be "put on the spot." He will resent and shrink from anything that might tend to minimize him as an individual.

Because a teen-ager likes to feel needed, he is elated when he can do something helpful. He is hungry for approval, and thrills to and thrives on words of discreet praise that reward him for his efforts.

A teen-ager will often talk over his problems with another adult rather than go to his parents for help or advice. Usually there are parent-offspring conflicts which arise because of opposing viewpoints and a lack of understanding. A teen-ager loves his parents and wants to feel the security of knowing that they love him. However, he thinks his parents still regard him as a child, and he feels he must break away from them and their seemingly unreasonable judgment in order to become an adult.

In times of trouble, the teen-ager frequently turns to a youth leader. The leader's role then is to guide the teen-ager in learning to improve and help himself; to see that he is thinking and approaching his tasks from the right direction; and to give suggestions and helpful guidance toward the solution of his problems or anxieties.

When making definite plans for a party or other social function, the teen-ager craves independence from adult interference. He wants to be in complete charge. This includes inviting guests, planning the menu, and arranging for entertainment. The parent or youth leader should offer guidance only. Teen-agers should be guided but not directed. Making mistakes is part of living and growing up. Teen-agers should be helped in making a choice, but the choice should not be made for them. Sometimes youth committees decide only "to have music and dance." To the parent or youth leader who hopes the party will be a success and enjoyed by all of the guests, this presents a delicate problem. The wise adult will accept this as typical, logical, and normal. He will not fail to be present the night of the party, however, ready to introduce a new activity should the party become too dull, sophisticated, or immature.

2 working with teen-agers

A teen-ager must develop a friendly personality that will attract others. He must learn to get along harmoniously with people, to respect authority and the feelings of others, to take disappointments without emotional outbursts, and to act according to his best convictions regardless of what others say. By working and planning cooperatively with the teen-ager, parents and youth leaders can help him find and know himself in relation to people and the community in which he lives.

When you conduct teen-age social or recreational functions, capture and keep the teen-ager's attention and interest. Recognize that teen-agers are bubbling with energy. Harness this vitality and direct the activities so that it is used wholesomely. Teen-agers attending a party or dance can sometimes make things difficult for the adult in charge. If the activities are not properly guided and controlled, it is easy for teen-agers to get out of step and hard to get the party back into the right pattern. Control is easiest if it functions from the very beginning.

Be ready on time. Girls are usually more anxious than boys to attend social functions and are always prompt, if not a little ahead of time. Boys generally file in later. The moment the guests arrive, give them something to do. Require that they all join in the activities. Accept no excuses or refusals. Cheerfully direct each one to the scene of the activity and explain briefly what he is to do. New arrivals see everyone occupied and join the fun without hesitation.

Do not attempt to give directions until you have the attention of the entire group. Expect the teen-ager to listen. Speak so that you can be heard, but do not shout. Be firm, but blend this firmness with kindness and gentleness.

That there be *no spectators* is another rule for teen-age parties. A boy sitting on the side line with his feet propped on a chair can demoralize the party completely. To cover his own shyness, he makes fun of the other guests' efforts. His wisecracks and noises are discouraging and disrupting to those taking part in the activity. When everyone is occupied, self-consciousness is replaced by enthusiasm for the game or activity.

Move quickly from one activity to another. Parties for teen-agers should be jam-packed with activity. They should not last too long—two to two-and-one-half hours is sufficient. Intermissions or coke breaks should be short. Do not try to compete with television, radio, ping pong, card games, or other amusements that might be going on in another room. This gives the teen-ager an excuse to meander away from the group. Insist that all guests remain in the room and participate in the planned activity.

When introducing a new game or dance, lead the group into the activity without their being conscious that they are being led. Never announce the nature of the next activity. (Right then some of the teen-agers might decide not to take part.)

Keeping the party moving is the secret of successful party management. The moment you become aware of fading interest, introduce a new activity *immediately*. Sustain interest. Have all the equipment you will need close at hand, and allow no lull between activities. Pauses are uninteresting and could result in losing the interest of the group. The party program should be flexible, and the leader should be prepared to make changes if the occasion demands.

Since the recognition a person gets for winning a game or contest is reward enough, the value of a prize is negligible. However, a token prize such as gum, individually wrapped pieces of candy, puzzles, tricks, and so on, that can be purchased in novelty shops, may be given. Centerpieces or decorations may also be used for this purpose.

Teen-age parties must have an adult present. Parents should welcome the guest and then retire to another room (unless they are assisting with the activities), but they should be nearby if needed. Start teen-age parties promptly and end them at the exact time stated on the invitation. Parents are expecting their sons and daughters home at a specific time and should not be subjected to unnecessary worry.

This may be the teen-ager's first party or dance. Youth leaders and parents can suggest many things to improve the teen-ager's social graces. For example, if the game requires a chair for each guest, ask each boy to get a chair for himself and one for his partner. Or, when the party is over, suggest that the guest express his thanks to the hostess or a member of the committee. For some teen-agers this takes courage. The parents or youth leader should be near the door ready to take his hand and say, "I'm glad you could come."

Parents usually brief their sons and daughters about what to do when they attend their first party. The courtesies mentioned are what every parent expects of his son and daughter. Teen-agers often forget, however, or are embarrassed or shy unless they are guided. No one is more grateful at the end of a well-planned party than the teen-agers themselves. This is apparent when they say with big smiles, "Gee, we had a lot of fun. Nancy is in my history class, but we never spoke to each other before tonight." Tactful suggestions by the leader throughout the evening bring out the best in these young people, who are trying so hard to be what adults want them to be. One little fellow remarked as he was leaving a party, "Gosh, I didn't know I could be so nice."

When teen-agers leave a party with this sense of well-being, there is no doubt—you have had a successful party.

3 pre-party activities

Start the teen-age party when the first guests arrive. The activities suggested in this chapter are not too highly organized; they serve the purpose of keeping early arrivals actively engaged while waiting for the rest of the group. There just is not time or opportunity for them to feel shy or ill at ease.

The games selected for pre-party activities must be governed by the amount of space you have and the type of clothing the teen-agers are wearing. A thirteen-year-old wearing "heels" would have difficulty if she were asked to participate in these types of activities. For "dress-up" teen-age parties the games in the next chapter would be more suitable.

If the occasion is a picnic, school party, or church function, where the teen-agers are dressed casually, do plan pre-party activities, because they always get the teen-age party off to a good controlled start.

The games described in this chapter are played in circle formation, which makes it easy for a newcomer to join the group as soon as he arrives. If the circle exceeds twenty to twenty-five players, start another circle. Form as many circles as needed. Be sure that everyone is included in the pre-party activities. If two or more circles are formed, each circle can be playing a different game. Rotate the equipment so that each circle plays several games.

These games help to fill in the time until everyone arrives. As soon as the majority are present, start the other activities.

jump the rope

NUMBER OF PLAYERS—Six to twenty-five players per circle.

MATERIALS NEEDED—Stout rope 15′ to 20′ long. Old sneaker or light object.

Tie an old sneaker (or some other lightweight object) to the end of a long rope.

Players form a circle, with one person on the inside. The inside person is "It" and must swing the rope around so that the shoe on the end of the rope passes under the feet of the players standing around forming the circle.

As the shoe is swung under the players' feet, each player must jump. The player who fails to jump the rope, and gets twisted in the rope, must go into the center and take "It's" place.

NOTE TO THE LEADER

The player in the center must swing the rope so that the shoe is in contact with the floor at all times.

If you care to make this an elimination game, have the players who fail to jump the rope leave the ring. But give them something else to do—act as judges, cheer for their favorites, not just wander off.

howdy!

NUMBER OF PLAYERS—Six to twenty-five players per circle.
MATERIALS NEEDED—None.

Players stand in a large circle, about an arm's length apart. One player is "It." He skips around the outside of the circle and taps one of the players on the shoulder. After tapping the player, "It" continues to skip around the circle. The player who was tapped leaves his place and skips around the circle in the *opposite* direction.

When players meet each other, they must stop and bow, shake hands, and say "howdy" before continuing back to the vacant spot in the circle. The first player to reach the vacant spot steps into the space and is safe. The other player continues as "It."

straddle ball

NUMBER OF PLAYERS—Ten to twenty-five players per circle.
MATERIALS NEEDED—Volleyball or beach ball.

The players stand in a large circle, feet spread far apart so that they touch their neighbors' feet. One person is chosen to go to the center of the circle. "It" has a ball which he attempts to roll between the legs of the players standing in the circle. He moves around quickly and tries to catch the players in the circle "off guard." Players may use only their *hands* to stop the ball from going between their legs.

Any player who allows the ball to pass between his legs, changes places with the person in the center and becomes the next "It."

pick up and dodge ball

NUMBER OF PLAYERS—Six to twenty-five players per circle.
MATERIALS NEEDED—Volleyball or beach ball; five paper swatters or other objects.

Arrange the players in a circle. Select one player to be "It." Scatter four or five paper swatters on the floor inside the ring. The players on the outside of the circle throw the ball, attempting to hit the player on the inside. "It" attempts to pick up the swatters and at the same time tries to avoid being hit with the ball. He may pick up only *one* swatter at a time.

If the ball goes out of bounds, "It" must wait until the ball is recovered and brought back into the circle before he can pick up another swatter. If a player hits "It," he goes to the center and takes "It's" place. If "It" is successful in picking up all the swatters, he chooses another player to take his place.

bird in a cage

NUMBER OF PLAYERS—Any number, divided into groups of three or four.
MATERIALS NEEDED—None.

Three or four players hold hands in a small circle to form a bird's cage. A player stands in the center of this circle of joined hands to be the bird. There can be any number of bird cages, and these should be dotted around the playing area. One person is chosen to be the bird *without* a cage ("It"). The leader blows a whistle or calls out, "Birds Fly!" On this signal, all birds duck under the joined hands of the players forming the circle and find a new cage. The bird who fails to find a cage is "It." Occasionally shift, so that all players will have a chance to be a bird.

dodge ball

NUMBER OF PLAYERS—Six to twenty-five players per circle.
MATERIALS NEEDED—Volleyball or beach ball.

The players stand in a large circle. Three or more players are chosen to go into the center of the circle. The players standing around the outside of the circle attempt to hit the players on the inside with the ball. Those inside may dodge, jump, or avoid the ball in any other way except by going out of the circle.

Any player who hits a dodger goes into the center and takes the place of the player who was hit. The "ousted" dodger joins the players in the outside circle. Individual players remain in the ring until they are hit by a ball. If a player is hit by a ball thrown by a person who has stepped inside the circle, he is not out.

circle kick ball

NUMBER OF PLAYERS—Ten to twenty-five players per circle.

MATERIALS NEEDED—Soft ball or other light object.

Players stand in a large circle with hands joined. A *soft* ball (or a knotted towel) is placed in the center of the circle. On the "Go" signal, players attempt to kick the ball out of the ring. The ball must pass *under* the joined hands of the other players. Players must keep hands joined at all times and use only their feet to stop the ball.

If the ball leaves the ring by passing to the right of any individual player or between his legs, the player who kicked the ball scores one point. The ball is recovered and returned to the center of the circle each time a point is scored. Play is then resumed. The player with the highest score at the end of the game is declared the winner.

One point will be subtracted from the score of any player who kicks the ball so that it passes *over* the joined hands of the other players.

swat tag

NUMBER OF PLAYERS—Six to twenty-five players per circle.

MATERIALS NEEDED—One paper swatter. (Roll four double sheets of newspaper together; tape to keep them from unrolling.)

The players stand in a circle with hands behind backs. One player, who is "It," walks around the outside of the circle carrying a paper swatter. "It" places the swatter in the hands of a player who is standing in the circle and takes that person's place, standing in the circle with the rest of the players.

The player who receives the swatter turns to the person on his *right.* He begins to swat at and chase him around the circle until the runner is back to his original place. (The chaser must swat the runner on the hips and not on any other part of the body.)

If the chaser is able to catch and swat the runner, the runner becomes the new "It." Should the chaser fail to swat the runner, he continues as "It."

4 games for getting acquainted

For a home party or any other social function where the space is limited, do not have guests just sit and wait for the others to arrive. A good shock absorber for a shy teen-ager is a glass of punch, followed by something to keep him occupied.

Have a jigsaw puzzle spread out on a card table, a take-it-apart puzzle on the coffee table, a set of indoor quoits set up in one end of the room, a box of toothpicks and a bottle placed on a table to see how many toothpicks can be stacked on top of it, or some of the games and gadgets left over from Christmas. The teen-agers will just naturally be attracted to these points of interest and be contented with them until the rest of the guests arrive and it is time to start the other activities.

guess what?

NUMBER OF PLAYERS—Any number.

MATERIALS NEEDED—A pencil and a GUESS WHAT? contest sheet for each person (sample sheet on next page).

To set everyone at ease, try this guessing game, which is guaranteed to keep the early arrivals occupied.

Place the following materials on a large table in the center of the room: (1) jar of beans; (2) rope 6 to 8 feet long; (3) eight comic strip (or baby) pictures, each pasted on a separate piece of cardboard and numbered; (4) heavy stone or brick; (5) rice, beans, or anything else that rattles, inside a box which is gift wrapped; (6) eight bottles with tops (these can be purchased reasonably at any drugstore). Number each bottle and place a small amount of vinegar, iodine, turpentine, water, and other liquids in the numbered bottles.

Give each player a pencil and a carbon copy of the GUESS WHAT? question sheet. Instruct them to *count*, *measure*, *lift*, *sniff*, and then write their answers in the proper blanks. After a reasonable amount of time has been allowed for them to inspect the materials on the table, read the correct answers and award the winner of each contest a prize.

NOTE TO THE LEADER

Be sure to prepare a master sheet so that you can announce the correct answers at the end of the contest. As you read the correct answers, the players may check their own papers.

(Sample Sheet)

GUESS WHAT?

Name ________________________ Prizes to the winners.

Count! Measure! Lift! Sniff!

Write the correct answers in the proper blank.

1

How many beans are in the jar?

____

4

What is the weight?

______lbs. ______oz.

2

How many inches long is the rope?

______inches

5

What is in the box?

____

3

Write the names of the people in the pictures.

1. ____________________
2. ____________________
3. ____________________
4. ____________________
5. ____________________
6. ____________________
7. ____________________
8. ____________________

6

Open the bottles. Sniff! What is in each bottle?

1. ____________________
2. ____________________
3. ____________________
4. ____________________
5. ____________________
6. ____________________
7. ____________________
8. ____________________

Keep this paper. The correct answers will be announced.

who's who?

NUMBER OF PLAYERS—Any number.

MATERIALS NEEDED—A pencil and a WHO'S WHO? contest sheet for each person (sample sheet on next page).

This is an entertaining way to start a party. Guests mingle and talk to each other without formal introductions. As each arrives, give him a pencil and a carbon copy of the WHO'S WHO? contest sheet.

The object of the game is to fill in the squares with people's names and each one's favorite color. To secure these names, the player moves around the room and visits with another player briefly. He writes this person's name and favorite color in one of the squares and then goes on to another person.

After a reasonable length of time has been allowed for the players to secure the names of one another, the leader requests all to sit down in a circle. The remaining part of the game is conducted like *bingo*. The leader, by looking at the name tag or referring to a list, announces the name of a player. This player stands up. The player who has this person's name written on his paper, puts a large X in that square. The leader continues to announce names until someone has five X's in a row. They may be up and down, across, or diagonal. This person calls *bingo* and is awarded a prize.

NOTE TO THE LEADER

Instead of asking the person his favorite color, make the question one that will stimulate conversation in the particular group being entertained. School or church

(Sample Sheet)

WHO'S WHO?

Shake hands and say "hello" to a guest. Write his or her name and favorite color in one of the squares. Visit with this person for a minute or two, then go to another guest and get the same information. Fill all the squares. When you have finished, keep this paper. The WINNER of the contest will be announced later.

		Your name Favorite color		

affiliation, home town, or place of birth could be the subjects of questions.

This is an excellent way for teen-agers to get acquainted when they are attending youth conferences where there are representatives from different schools, towns, or states. They carry this WHO'S WHO? sheet with them. At a dinner or some other social event the names of the different players are read. Collecting names, home towns, and schools makes a perfect opportunity for speaking to an unknown teen-ager.

At a gathering where the players are walking around to get this information, it is easier for them to write if each WHO'S WHO? sheet is stapled to a heavy piece of cardboard or printed on a file card.

This contest is most effective when the group is fairly large in number.

gussy gossip

NUMBER OF PLAYERS—Any number.
MATERIALS NEEDED—A pencil and a GUSSY GOSSIP sheet for each guest (sample sheet on next page).

This is an excellent ice-breaker and a good pastime to keep the early guests occupied while waiting for a few others.

As each guest enters, give him a pencil and a copy of the GUSSY GOSSIP sheet. Guests circulate through the room seeking correct answers to the questions, and each writes the correct person's name on his paper.

It's fun to listen to the different conversations: "Oh, I didn't know you had three brothers. When's your

(Sample Sheet)

GUSSY GOSSIP!

Shake hands and say hello to a guest. Ask him anything that might help you to find the correct answers to the questions asked below. Keep moving around, talking to as many guests as possible. Keep this paper when you have finished. The correct names will be announced.

Find the answer.	Write name here.
1. Who has the shortest last name?	
2. Who is the tallest person?	
3. Who has the most brothers?	
4. Who has the most sisters?	
5. Who had the last birthday?	
6. Who lives the farthest away?	
7. Who lives the closest?	
8. Who has the next birthday?	
9. Who has the longest first name?	
10. Who has the shortest first name?	

birthday? Where do you live?" In minutes everyone is engaged in friendly conversation.

After a reasonable amount of time has been allowed, the guests are asked to sit down. The leader announces the correct answers, and each guest corrects his own paper. If the question applied to more than one person, credit is given for both answers. The person having the most correct list of names is awarded a prize.

NOTE TO THE LEADER

Make a list of the correct names so that you can announce them.

last name scrabble

NUMBER OF PLAYERS—Any number.

MATERIALS NEEDED—Name tags, a pencil and a LAST NAME SCRABBLE sheet for each person. (Sample sheet on next page.)

This hunting game, like several others mentioned in this chapter, provides a means of keeping early teenagers pleasantly occupied until the others arrive at the party.

Give each guest a pencil and a copy of the LAST NAME SCRABBLE sheet. Each player prints his *first* and *last* name on the lines going down the left-hand side of the paper. Players move about, finding persons whose last names begin with the letters in their name. The finder will say hello to this person before writing the newly discovered guest's name on his list.

A person's name may be used only once unless there are two or more guests present who have the same

(Sample Sheet)

LAST NAME SCRABBLE

Print your first and last name on the lines going down the LEFT-hand side of the paper. Move around. Shake hands and say "hello" to the persons you find whose LAST names begin with the letters in your name. Write their names on your sheet in the correct spaces next to the letters of your own name. Hand in your paper when you have finished.

Print your name	Name of player whose LAST NAME starts with this letter	Player's first name

last name. Following is an example using Mary Brown's name:

M	–	Miller	Kay
A	–	Arnold	Bill
R	–	Ross	Lillian
Y	–	Young	Patricia
B	–	Baker	Pete
R	–	Ramsey	Jim
O	–	Owens	Lucille
W	–	Walker	Mary
N	–	Nunes	Barbara

NOTE TO THE LEADER

Award a prize to the guest who is first to finish the contest. You may wish also to award a prize to the persons with the longest and shortest names.

5 mixers

The first step in getting party guests acquainted is to place squares of paper and a few magic markers on a table near the entrance. Ask each person to print his first and last name and pin the name tag on his left lapel. (Be sure the names are printed in large letters.) Use name tags, even if you do think everyone knows everyone else. There will nearly always be a few who won't.

Many shy teen-agers find it difficult to approach and speak to a stranger. They like to be introduced. A reception line does not take long, and it will put the guests in a party mood. Even if most of them do know each other, there is something about a handshake and a friendly hello that creates a feeling of warmth and good fellowship.

how to form a reception line

Members of the welcoming committee or the hosts stand at the front of the room. All others form a single line, so that the first person in the guest line is in a position to shake the hand of the first person in the welcoming group.

After these two shake hands and exchange a few words of greeting, guest number *one* stands on the far side of the person whose hand he has just shaken. He is now a part of the welcoming line and remains in this position ready to greet the next guest. Guest number *two* follows directly behind guest number *one*. After guest number two has shaken hands with guest number one, he joins the welcoming line by standing on the far side of guest number one. He too remains here to greet the other guests. (Name tags are a quick means of identification in this situation.)

Each person, in turn, moves down the line shaking hands and after shaking the last person's hand, steps into line and stands ready to greet the people who were behind him.

NOTE TO THE LEADER

The purpose of the reception line is just to provide a handshake and a quick hello. Keep the line moving, so that the teen-agers will not become restless. Those who wish to carry on long conversations can do so later.

Continue the line until every one has met everyone else. If the reception line is too long or too much time is being consumed, discontinue the greetings after the original members of the welcoming committee have had an opportunity to welcome each guest.

A reception line is a wonderful aid to a party host. It assures him that everyone will meet everyone else, and it's an activity in which all take part. It creates a friendly feeling, brings the group together, and—while all the guests are standing—presents a wonderful opportunity for the leader to begin another activity in which all can participate.

Good follow-up activities to use after the reception line (while everyone is still standing) are mixers.

Mixers should be used early in the program. They help teen-agers to relax and chase away any shyness or self-consciousness they may be suffering from.

The instructions for any game or contest classified as a mixer always require each individual to seek a partner or join a specific group. Players are then assigned something to do that must be accomplished together. Immediately everyone has the feeling of belonging, and creating this feeling is the secret of any successful social gathering.

Mixers always mean a change of partners; partners are usually separated. In many respects this is good. If the boyfriend is reluctant about joining the activities, he cannot very well ask someone he has just met to "sit this one out." When the mixer is over, he returns to his partner all ready to join her in the next activity.

pantomimes

Chance determines who will be partners in this exciting game. After it, there may be some question as to whether all the players are entirely sound mentally!

Prepare two sets of the following pantomime subjects (put each pantomime on a separate slip of paper):

1. Napoleon
2. Tightrope Walker
3. Swimmer
4. Tennis Player
5. Opera Singer
6. Check-Out Clerk
7. Someone Burping Baby
8. Indian Dancer
9. Piano Teacher
10. Bus Driver
11. Doctor
12. Political Speaker
13. Hunter
14. Mechanical Doll
15. Skater
16. Monkey
17. Accordion Player
18. Elephant
19. Water Skier
20. Astronaut
21. Golfer
22. Rabbit
23. Trumpet Player
24. Cowboy
25. Football Player
26. Window Washer
27. Butterfly Catcher
28. Great Lover
29. Tap Dancer
30. Lion Tamer

Distribute one set of the pantomimes to the girls and the duplicate set to the boys. The object of the game is for each person to find his or her partner *without speaking a word.*

When the game starts, each player circulates through the room, continually acting out his pantomime. When one player finds someone he *suspects* might have the same pantomime as his, he acts his part especially for this person. The second person likewise does the pantomime assigned to him. If these two are doing the same pantomime, they are partners and walk around the outside of the room doing their pantomime together. Partners continue to walk together until everyone has found his or her partner.

NOTE TO THE LEADER

Collect the slips of paper after the players have read their assignments.

you're my friend

This mixer provides an excellent way for young teen-agers to get acquainted.

The chairs are arranged in a circle, one chair for each person. The boys are asked to leave the room. Girls move so that there is an empty chair to everyone's right. The leader gives each girl a slip of paper with a number on it. This is the number of her "special" friend. For example, if her number is 3, then the third boy to come into the room is her "special" friend.

While the boys are in another room, the leader gives each boy a duplicate number of the ones he gave the girls. The boys will be called into the room where the girls are, one by one, according to the number each holds. The object of the game for each girl is to get the boy who is her special friend to sit down on the vacant chair at her right.

When the first player from the outside is admitted, the girls seated in the circle immediately start shouting, "You are my friend and this is your chair. You are my friend and this is your chair." Each girl does her best to get the boy to sit down beside her. All kinds of salesmanship can and will be used: shouting, pointing, pleading hands, knee bending, sobs, etc.

Finally the boy will choose a seat. If it's the wrong one, he is booed by the girls and has to sit on the floor. The next boy is called in and, after he gets the treatment, chooses a seat. If it is the right one, he remains in that chair. After all the boys have had a chance to find their partners, the ones who were not successful the first time may try again. The game continues until everyone has discovered his special friend.

we're a pair

Here is a simple but very effective way to arrange a group of people into couples or pairs.

Arrange two decks of old playing cards in exactly the same order. Be sure you have one card for each guest. Distribute the cards from one deck to the girls and the duplicate cards of the other deck to the boys. The object of the game is for each person to find his or her *partner*.

When the signal to start is given, each person circulates and looks for the person holding the same card that he is holding. When two people holding the same card find each other, these two are partners. (Example: The boy and the girl holding the Ace of Hearts are partners.) When they locate each other, they link arms and walk around the outside of the room. Couples continue to walk together until all have found partners.

VARIATION

Distribute the cards to the boys and girls. After they have looked at their cards, collect the cards. Without saying a word, the players pantomime the *number* and *suit* of their card until they find their partners.

mystery guest

NUMBER OF PLAYERS—Any number.
MATERIALS NEEDED—Name tags; an inexpensive prize.

Mystery engages the imagination and spurs the interest. This game is an entertaining way for people to get acquainted without shyness or hesitation.

One of the players (unknown to any of the others) is selected to be the MYSTERY GUEST. Players are instructed to move around the room, shake hands and say hello to as many people as possible. The MYSTERY GUEST mingles with the group and shakes hands with as many persons as he can. However, he keeps track of the number of people who approach him voluntarily. The *fifteenth* person to shake the MYSTERY GUEST's hand is the lucky person who receives the prize. The leader introduces the winning person to the group and discloses the identity of the MYSTERY GUEST.

match me

If the next activity is to be a couple game, here is an easy way to get the group paired off.

Cut small squares of cloth or paper, two of each color or pattern. Place one of each in separate boxes. Pass one box to the boys and the other to the girls. Boys and girls having matching colors or patterns are partners.

paper handshake

NUMBER OF PLAYERS –Any number.

MATERIALS NEEDED–Name tags; a paper bag for each guest.

Here is another very effective way to stimulate friendliness, have a lot of fun, get everyone acquainted in an informal way, and put the players into a party mood.

As each person arrives, the leader presents him with a paper bag and instructs him to place it over his right hand. Players move around the room greeting and shaking hands with as many others as possible.

A prize is awarded to the first person to wear out his or her paper bag–not by tearing, but by shaking hands.

NOTE TO THE LEADER

A rubber band around the wrist helps to hold the paper bag in place.

whistle stop

NUMBER OF PLAYERS—Any number.
MATERIALS NEEDED—Name tags; whistle.

This is a good way to help teen-agers get acquainted in a very informal way.

Players stand in a large circle while the leader gives the instructions. One blast of the whistle means to form one large circle. If there are five blasts, five players must group together. Then before the whistle is sounded again, each person in this group of five will say "Hi" and name the four other people in the group. When the whistle blows, this group separates. The number of blasts from the leader's whistle indicates the number of people who are to group together.

NOTE TO THE LEADER

This is an easy method to use for organizing a group of people and getting them into groups of equal size.

mixer for shy teen-agers

The following is a way of mixing a large group of young teen-agers if you think they tend to be shy.

The teen-ager's reason for coming to the party in the first place, although he or she would not admit it, is to be in the company of the opposite sex. If you suggest, however, that a boy ask a girl to be his partner, half the boys might seek refuge in the boys' room. Don't let them know, therefore, that they are about to be paired off. Merely ask the boys to stand in a line on one side of the room and the girls to line up on the opposite side, facing the boys. Then ask both lines to face the front of the room. Start some music. Instruct the first boy and the first girl to walk toward the center of the room. When they meet, they are to join hands and go down the center of the floor together. The other boys and girls will follow.

When the teen-agers first pair up, you hear shouts of glee, shrieks of horror, and deep mumbling sounds from the boys. These are actually expressions of delight. You would not know from the sounds, but this is what they have been waiting for. The evening is beginning to be a success.

After one of these mixers has put the teen-agers in pairs, do something that can be explained briefly and accomplished easily. It is not long before the teen-ager discovers he is not so shy, dumb, or awkward as he thought. He also finds that having a girl for a partner is really fun. Once the teen-ager gets this satisfied feeling, the rest of the program is smooth sailing for the youth leader or parent.

6 party contests

This series of contests places every teen-ager on a team. Teams compete with each other to see which can accumulate the highest number of points. A prize is awarded to each member of the winning team at the end of the contests.

A scorekeeper to keep the accumulative score and two judges to referee and assist the leader are appointed. Each time one of the contests is won by a team or members of a team, the scorekeeper credits that team with 5 points.

To organize the group for the following contests, divide the players in half and have them sit, boys and girls alternating, on rows of chairs facing each other. In some of the contests all team members are required to stand in order to compete with the other team. In other contests the leader selects a number of players from each team to compete against each other while their seated teammates cheer and encourage the contestants to do their very best for the glory of their team.

If possible there should be fifteen to twenty feet distance between the two rows of chairs, or lines of players, to serve as the playing area. For convenience one team will be referred to as the *red* team and the other as the *blue* team.

NOTE TO THE LEADER

These competitive contests can be used with small or very large groups of teen-agers. If the group is large, start the activity from both ends of the line when possible. In the passing games, give each player the object to be passed and instruct all the players to pass the object received toward the center. The first team to have the objects meet, near the center of the line, is declared the winner. This method takes only half as much time and keeps the contest from dragging.

Red Team	O O O O O O O O O O
	Playing Area
Blue Team	X X X X X X X X X X

The instructions for each contest tell how many players are required. In many instances, individual players or groups of players are called upon to compete for their team. Try to use every person on the teams in at least one of these contests.

bend your elbow

NUMBER OF PLAYERS—Any number, divided into two equal teams.

MATERIALS NEEDED—Two potatoes, small balls, or any objects which may be passed from one person to another.

Players stand in front of their chairs for this contest. The players on the red team stand facing the players on the blue team.

Each player bends both arms upward, making a trough with his arms and elbows. The leader places a potato between the elbows of the first player on each team. On the signal "Go," the first player turns to the second player and drops the potato into the crook of the second player's upturned arms. The second player passes to the third, and so on.

If the potato is dropped, the last person to touch it picks it up, replaces it between his elbows, and continues to pass the potato down the line. The team to finish first is declared the winner.

Award the winning team 5 points.

ankle pass

NUMBER OF PLAYERS—Any number, divided into two equal teams.

MATERIALS NEEDED—Two potatoes, small balls, or any objects which may be passed from one person to another.

Players on the red team sit on chairs facing the players on the blue team. All players put their feet together and turn their toes up.

The leader places a potato on the insteps of the first player in each line. On the signal "Go," the first player, using only his feet, drops the potato onto the insteps of the second player. The second player passes to the third, and so on.

If the potato rolls to the floor, it is recovered by the person who dropped it and is replaced on his insteps, and the contest continues. As soon as the last player on either team receives the potato, the race ends and his team is declared winner.

Award the winning team 5 points.

balloon bounce

NUMBER OF PLAYERS—One boy from each team.
MATERIALS NEEDED—Two overcoats or jackets; two bottles of pop; twenty matches for each player; two inflated balloons.

One boy from each team is chosen to do this feat. These two boys come to the center of the playing area and stand some distance apart. The leader gives each boy a balloon and an overcoat. A bottle of pop for each player is placed on the floor, and twenty matches are scattered around each boy.

The player's job is to keep the balloon bouncing in the air with one hand while he puts on the overcoat, drinks the pop, and picks up all the matches. If the balloon touches the floor at any time, the player must remove the overcoat, scatter all of the matches on the floor and start again. The player to complete this task first is declared the winner.

Award the winning team 5 points.

chinny chin chin

NUMBER OF PLAYERS—Any number, divided into two equal teams.
MATERIALS NEEDED—Two inflated balloons.

Players stand in front of their chairs for this contest. The players on the red team stand facing the players on the blue team. An inflated balloon is placed under the chin of the first player in each line. The player lowers his chin so that he can hold the balloon in this position without the use of his hands.

On the signal "Go," the first player turns to the second player. The second player, *without the use of his hands*, takes the balloon with his *chin* from the first person. He in turn passes the balloon on to the third person, and so on.

If the balloon is dropped in the process of being passed from chin to chin, there are two alternative rules:

1. Allow the person who last had the balloon to recover it, place it under his chin with his hands, and then pass it on to the next person.
2. Require the player who dropped the balloon to recover it from the floor with his chin.

NOTE TO THE LEADER

Have a few extra inflated balloons ready. Replace any broken balloons quickly.

Award the winning team 5 points.

potato race

NUMBER OF PLAYERS—Two teams, three girls and three boys on each team.

MATERIALS NEEDED—Two teaspoons; two potatoes.

Three girls from the red team stand one behind the other at one end of the floor. Three boys from the red team stand one behind the other at the opposite end of the floor. The players from the blue team line up the same way.

The leader gives the first girl on each team a teaspoon and a potato. On the signal "Go," the first girl balances the the potato on the teaspoon, runs across the room, and hands the spoon and the potato to the first boy on her team. She then goes to the end of the boys' line. The first boy balances the potato on the spoon and runs across the room to the second girl. The boy goes to the end of the girls' line. Should a player drop the potato, he must recover it, replace it on the spoon, and continue to run. The team to finish first is declared the winner.

Award the winning team 5 points.

ski race

NUMBER OF PLAYERS—Two teams, three boys and three girls from each team.

MATERIALS NEEDED—Four paper plates or pieces of cardboard 8½ by 11 inches.

Three girls from the red team stand one behind the other, single file at one end of the floor. Three boys from the red team stand one behind the other, single file, at the opposite end of the floor. The players from the blue team line up the same way.

The leader places two pieces of cardboard on the floor in front of the first girl on each team. On the signal "Go," the first girl steps onto the cardboard and uses them like skis. She shuffles, or "skis," across the floor to the first boy on her team, and steps off the cardboard. She then goes to the end of the boys' line. The first boy mounts the skis and shuffles across the floor to the second girl on his team. He steps off the cardboard and goes to the end of the girls' line. When the contest ends, all of the boys are on the girls' side of the floor and vice versa.

Should a player lose his skis while shuffling, he must run back to recover them. After he mounts them again, he may continue on his way. The team to finish first is declared the winner.

Award the winning team 5 points.

rainy washday

NUMBER OF PLAYERS—Two teams, eight players on each team.

MATERIALS NEEDED—Two clotheslines; old clothing; plenty of clothespins.

Players line up one behind the other for this contest.

About thirty feet away from the teams, have two people hold a clothesline full of pinned-up clothing. On the signal "Go," each team sends the first player to *take the clothing down.* These players run back and hand the clothing and pins to the second player. The second player runs to the clothesline and *hangs the clothing on the line.* The third player removes the clothing from the line, and so on. The first team to finish wins the contest.

Award the winning team 5 points.

NOTE TO THE LEADER

This is amusing to those who are watching. Players will have difficulty holding the clothespins, and the fellows—perhaps not accustomed to hanging clothes on a line—will be amusing.

spelling contest

NUMBER OF PLAYERS—Two teams, ten players on each team.

MATERIALS NEEDED—One of the following five-inch-high letters for each player: C O N S T A I P L E (red ink), C O N S T A I P L E (blue ink).

If there is a long line of players, the ten players from each team taking part in this SPELLING CONTEST will sit on the end chairs so that they are diagonally opposite each other.

Each player is given a card with a letter printed on it. The red letters are distributed to the players on the red team. The blue letters are given to the members of the blue team. The leader announces a word. The object of the game is to see which team can be first to spell this word correctly.

When a word is announced, a player having a letter needed to spell this word goes as quickly as possible to the end of the play area nearest to where he is sitting. He holds his letter chest high and stands in the right position to help spell this word correctly. For example: If the leader calls the word "cat," the players with the letters C, A, and T hurry to the designated place. Each holds his letter in front of his chest, and together they spell the word "cat."

The judges and the scorekeeper stand in a position so that they can see both lines of spellers. The judges decide which team was first to spell the word. The scorekeeper credits a team with *one point* for every word they are first to spell correctly. When the judges have designated the winner, all players go back to their seats, and the leader announces another word.

NOTE TO THE LEADER

The following is a suggested list of words to use for the SPELLING CONTEST. Start with short words and gradually make the words longer. These words are arranged in groups. If the complete group is used, each player will have a chance to participate in spelling a word. (As a variation, have the players spell the words backwards.)

3 Letters	4 Letters	5 Letters	6 Letters
cat	lean	noise	social
one	coat	coast	police
sip	spin	plate	notice
lap	nice	steal	places
cot	leap	point	
ale	stop	place	
sin	nest	alone	
pit	lice	clips	
can	soap	stone	
set			
lip			
toe			

sit down volley ball

NUMBER OF PLAYERS—Any number, divided into two equal teams.

MATERIALS NEEDED—Twelve to twenty inflated balloons.

Players sit in two long rows of chairs facing each other. The chairs should be close enough together so that the knees of the red team players are almost touching the knees of the players on the blue team. A goalkeeper for each team sits at left end of each line, in much the same position as a basket at the end of a basketball court. The leader appoints a timekeeper. The object of the game is to see which team can score the most points in the appointed time.

By batting the balloons with their hands, the players keep the balloons in the air and try to get them into the hands of their goalkeeper. Each team, of course, is trying to bat the balloons in the opposite direction. The red team players bat the balloons in the direction of the red goal. At the same time, the players on the blue team are trying to bat the balloons toward the blue goal. The goalkeeper keeps the score. He counts one point for each balloon he catches. The game has only one rule: *Players cannot stand up to bat the balloons.*

Here's how to get the game into action. The leader stands behind one row of chairs, close to the center. He starts the game by tossing a balloon into the air between the two rows of players. Players then attempt to bat the balloon toward their goal. When the players understand what they are to do, the leader puts several more balloons into play. He continues to toss balloons into the center of the two rows of chairs until all twenty balloons are in action.

Any balloons that are knocked out of bounds are recovered and put back into play between two people nearest the spot where the balloon went out of bounds. The balloons that the goalkeepers have caught (and counted) are collected and put into play again at the center.

At the end of the playing time, each goalkeeper announces the number of balloons he was able to catch. The team with the highest number of points is declared the winner.

Award the winning team 5 points.

NOTE TO THE LEADER

Appoint a couple of helpers to stand behind each row of chairs and assist in recovering the balloons that are knocked out of bounds. When the helpers recover a balloon, they will toss it between the two players sitting nearest the spot where it went out of bounds.

VARIATION

Instead of having the "goalie" catch the balloons, arm him with a straight pin. He would then keep track of the number of balloons he is able to break.

store

NUMBER OF PLAYERS—Any number.
MATERIALS NEEDED—Letters of the alphabet on large cards.

Players on the red team sit facing the players on the blue team. Players compete individually, each with the person sitting across from him.

The first players from each team stand and face the leader. The leader instructs them to call out the name of an article that can be found in the type of place he might mention and that starts with the letter on the card. (If he holds up the letter B and says, "grocery store," the answer could be bananas.) The player who is first to call out correctly the name of an article earns one point for his team. These two players sit down, and the next two players take their places. The game continues until each person has had a chance to name an article.

The leader flashes a different letter each time and changes the place; that is, he might mention a drugstore, hardware store, home, school, part of an automobile, etc.

Award the winning team 5 points.

draw a picture

NUMBER OF PLAYERS—Any number, divided into two teams.

MATERIALS NEEDED—Two large pieces of paper (36 by 36 inches); two magic markers or two heavy crayons.

The two large pieces of paper are placed on the wall in front of each team, so that they can be plainly seen by all of the players. Teams sit on opposite sides of the room facing the drawing boards.

By using the *joint efforts* of all its members, each team is instructed to draw a barnyard scene. The first person on each team is given the magic marker or heavy crayon. Players go one at a time to the drawing board and draw just one article which might be found in a barnyard—for example, a chicken, fence, barn, cow, cat, pitchfork, haystack, or whatever he may choose to draw. This is not a race, but no one person should take longer than 45 seconds to draw his one item.

The first person returns to his seat and hands the crayon to the second person on his team. The second person goes to the drawing board and adds his artistic touch to the picture. When all the players have had an opportunity to draw a part of the picture, the judge selects the better drawing.

Award the team with the best picture 5 points.

NOTE TO THE LEADER

If appropriate wall space is not available, scotch-tape the paper to the tops of two card tables. Collapse the legs and place the tables on the seats of two chairs. This arrangement makes very suitable drawing boards.

horse race

NUMBER OF PLAYERS—Two teams, three girls on each team.

MATERIALS NEEDED—Six pieces of cardboard, 8½ by 11 inches. Number each: 1, 2, 3 in red letters, 4, 5, 6 in blue letters. A disc divided into six equal parts and numbered 1, 2, 3 in red ink, 4, 5, 6 in blue ink.

Players from both teams stand side by side at the starting line, as horses line up for a race.

Give the players on the red team the cardboards numbered 1, 2, and 3. Numbers 4, 5, and 6 are distributed to the players on the blue team. Each player holds her number in front of her chest so that it can readily be seen. The leader establishes a finish line about twenty-five feet away from the starting line. The object of the game is to see which player will be first to step over the finish line. A player advances by taking *one big step forward* each time her number is called.

The leader stands facing the players at the finish line and spins the disc. (A hole is punched in the center of the disc, large enough to insert a pencil.) The leader spins the disc on the pencil and stops the spinning with his fingers. The number his finger is touching when the disc stops is the number of the player who takes one big step forward. The leader continues to spin the disc. He calls the lucky number each time he stops the disc, and waits until the player has taken her step forward before he spins again. The player who succeeds in stepping over the finish line first is declared the winner and earns 5 points for her team.

Award the winning team 5 points.

NOTE TO THE LEADER

An old 78 rpm record makes an excellent disc. Paste white paper over the disc and divide it into sections.

The girls may wish to remove their shoes in order to be able to take larger steps. This is permissible.

Before starting the race, have the girls take a few practice steps. Impress upon them the importance of *big* steps.

balloon battle

NUMBER OF PLAYERS—Two teams, four boys on each team.

MATERIALS NEEDED—Four red balloons and four blue balloons, eight light swatters, 9″ long string for each balloon.

To make the swatters, roll four double sheets of newspaper together. Tape to keep them from unrolling.

Tie the inflated red balloons to the *back* of the belts of the players on the red team. Tie the blue balloons to the *back* of the belts of the contestants from the blue team. Give each player a paper swatter.

The leader calls all the contestants together in the center of the playing area and explains the following rules:

1. The object of the game is for the red team to break the balloons of the blue team and vice versa.

2. On the signal "Go," players will attempt to hit and break the balloons of the *opposite team* with the paper swatters. At the same time, each player tries to protect and keep his own balloon from being broken.

3. Players may move anywhere within the designated playing area.
4. When a contestant's balloon is broken, he is automatically *eliminated* and must sit down.
5. The contest continues until all the players on one team are eliminated.

Award the winning team 5 points.

NOTE TO THE LEADER

If the players go at this game too vigorously and it becomes rough, call the game to a halt after two minutes. The team that has the most unbroken balloons at the end of the two minutes is declared the winner.

ping-pong blow

NUMBER OF PLAYERS—Two teams, three players on each team.

MATERIALS NEEDED—A long table and a ping-pong ball.

The three red team players stand at one end of the table, and the blue team players stand at the opposite end.

The leader places a ping-pong ball in the center of the table. On the signal "Go," each team attempts to *blow* the ball off the opposite end of the table. No player may use his hands or any part of his body to propel the ball. The players may move around the table to get into a more advantageous spot from which to blow the ball, protect their end of the table, or blow the ball off the opponents' end of the table.

Each time a team is successful in blowing the ball off the opposite end of the table, they score one point. After a point is scored, the ball is placed in the center of the table again. If the ball rolls off the side of the table, the leader returns it to the center and play resumes. The first team to score five points wins the contest.

Award the winning team 5 points.

personal scavenger hunt

NUMBER OF PLAYERS—Any number, divided into two equal teams.

MATERIALS NEEDED—One large table.

The leader places a table between two rows of chairs, and the red team sits facing the blue team.

Red Team	O O O O O O O O O O O
	Table
Blue Team	X X X X X X X X X X X

The leader calls for the following articles, one at a time, to be placed on the table:

1. Brown Shoelace
2. Aspirin Tablet
3. Pocket Comb
4. White Glove
5. Wooden Pencil
6. Straight Pin
7. Cancelled Stamp
8. Rubber Band
9. White Hankie
10. Stick of Gum
11. Lady's Belt
12. White Sock
13. $1.00 Bill
14. Nail File
15. Paper Clip
16. Boy's Picture
17. Girl's Picture
18. Tie Clasp
19. Red Shoe
20. Man's Belt
21. Safety Pin
22. Pocket Knife
23. Bobby Pin
24. 5¢ Stamp

The object of the game is to see which individual on either the red or blue team can be first to place the item called for on the table. Any member of either team who has a *brown shoelace* immediately unlaces his or her shoe. He then makes a mad dash to the table, attempting to be the first to place his shoelace on the table.

The judge decides which player was first, and the scorekeeper keeps track of the number of points scored by each team. One point is scored for the team whose player placed his object on the table first. As soon as the judge has declared the winner, the articles are immediately returned to the owners. The players go back to their seats and wait for the leader to call for the next item.

NOTE TO THE LEADER

Players must have the article called for in their *hands* before starting to run to the table.

broom hockey

NUMBER OF PLAYERS—Two teams, five players on each team.

MATERIALS NEEDED—Two brooms and a sponge.

Five players from the red team sit facing five players from the blue team. The leader gives the players on each team a number (1, 2, 3, 4, 5). A sponge and two brooms are placed on the floor in the exact center of the two rows of chairs.

The object of the game is to *sweep* the sponge over the goal line. When the sponge is swept over the goal line by a player, his team scores one point.

The leader calls a number. Two players from opposite teams come to the center of the floor. They pick up a broom and stand facing their goal. The sponge is placed on the floor between the two players. On the

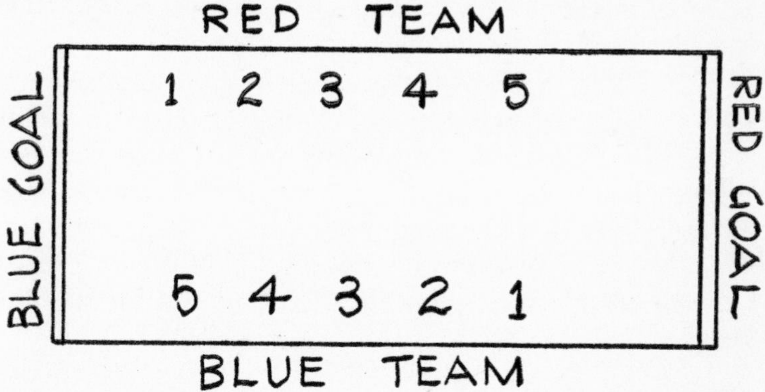

signal "Go," each player tries to sweep the sponge over his goal line. The players have one minute in which to score. If in that length of time neither player has made a goal, the leader declares it a tie and calls two other players to the center. Ten points win the game.

Award the winning team 5 points.

NOTE TO THE LEADER

Small children's brooms are fun to use for this game.

balloon sit

NUMBER OF PLAYERS—Two teams, two boys and one girl on each team.

MATERIALS NEEDED—Ten inflated balloons.

The leader places two chairs about five feet apart at one end of the room. A girl from the red team sits on one chair, and a girl from the blue team sits on the other.

A boy from each team stands behind the chair of the girl who is representing his team. The second boy from each team stands on the opposite side of the room and holds five balloons in his arms.

On the signal "Go," the boy standing behind the chair runs to the opposite end of the room. The boy standing there hands him *one* balloon. The runner then returns to the back of the chair where the girl is sitting. The girl momentarily stands up while the boy places the balloon on the seat of the chair. The girl *sits on the balloon,* attempting to break it. If she does not succeed the first time, she must keep trying until the balloon is broken. The balloon must not be held in place by either player. The boy runner waits until the girl breaks the balloon. He then runs to the opposite end of the room and returns with the second balloon, etc. The relay ends when all five balloons are broken.

The first team to break all five balloons is declared winner.

Award the winning team 5 points.

together we stand

NUMBER OF PLAYERS—Two couples, one couple representing each team.

MATERIALS NEEDED—Four pieces of heavy cord 45 inches long.

This is one of those pastimes that provide as much fun for the spectators as for the participants.

The object of the game is to have two people whose wrists have been tied together get separated without cutting or untying the cord. It can be done!

The leader ties one end of a piece of cord around the boy's right wrist and the other end around his left wrist. He ties a second piece of cord to the girl's right wrist, passes it behind the cord connecting the boy's wrists, then ties this end around the girl's left wrist. The two players are linked together (see illustration). The loops around the wrists must be just tight enough so that the players cannot slip the cords over their hands.

Tie one couple from the red team together and one couple from the blue team together. They will compete to see which couple can get untangled first. Allow five to ten minutes for the couples to attempt or accomplish this feat. If at the end of this time, neither couple has been able to get free, show them the solution. If one of the couples figured out the solution without help, they will be declared the winner.

Award the winning team 5 points.

NOTE TO THE LEADER

The contestants will go through all kinds of maneuvers. This is what makes it so amusing for the other players. The players will twist, turn, step, or even lie on the floor, but they will always end up as they started. Their teammates along the side line may wish to offer suggestions. This is fine *providing they do not know the real solution.*

The players may have twisted or knotted the cord while attempting to get separated. These twists must be undone before you can demonstrate how it could have been done. Be sure you have practiced the solution before you try it in public.

SOLUTION TO THE STRING GAME

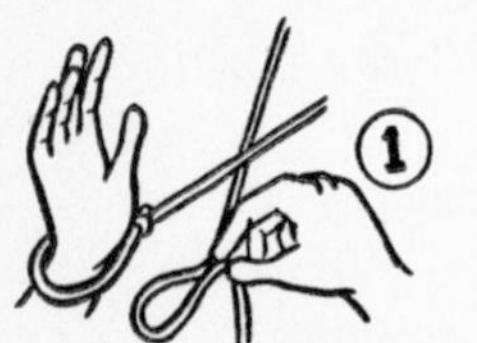

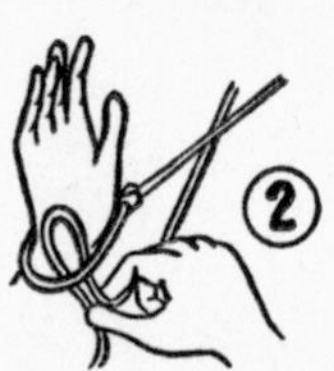

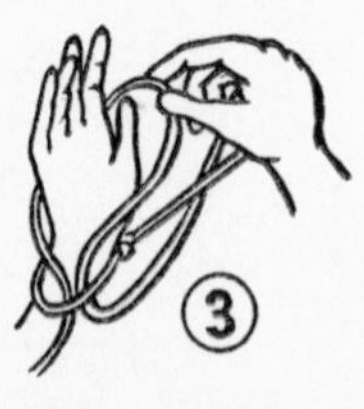

Have both players hold their arms as far apart as possible. The leader then grasps the bottom cord near the center and forms a loop. He slips this loop up under the cord that is tied around the opposite player's wrist. The loop is pulled up and slipped over the hand. The two players are then separated.

bowling game

NUMBER OF PLAYERS—Two teams, five players on each team.

MATERIALS NEEDED—Two balls, an empty milk carton as a target.

Five members of the red team sit facing five members of the blue team, with a distance of about twenty-five feet between the two teams.

A target is placed on the floor in the exact center of the two rows of chairs. A ball is placed on the floor in front of each team. The leader gives the players on each team a number (1, 2, 3, 4, 5).

The leader calls a number. The player on each team with that number stands, picks up the ball that is on the floor in front of his team, and rolls the ball at the target. The one who succeeds in knocking the target down scores one point for his team. If both players roll at the target and both fail to hit it, they recover the ball that was rolled by the opposite player, and try again to hit the target. These two players continue to roll at the target until one of the two succeeds in knocking the target over. After a point has been scored, the first two players go back to their seats. The target and balls are replaced, and the leader calls another number.

In the second round the players are required to *throw* the ball at the target. This makes it necessary to score a "direct hit" in order to earn a point. In the third round each player is instructed to *turn around*, bend forward, and roll the ball back between his feet to hit the target.

The first team to score fifteen points is declared the winner.

Award the winning team 5 points.

NOTE TO THE LEADER

Players must stay behind an established line when rolling the ball. If the player steps over the line, his score does not count.

For a more active game, when the player's number is called, have him run to the opposite side of the room. He picks up the ball that is on the floor in front of the opposite team and rolls it at the target. Players must continue to roll at the target until one of the players knocks it over. After the target is hit, the players return to their original sides.

egg walk

NUMBER OF PLAYERS—One boy and one girl from each team.

MATERIALS NEEDED—Four blindfolds; six hard-boiled eggs; twenty soda crackers; newspaper.

Place eggs here and there where the contestants can see them. Blindfold one boy and one girl from each team. Tell the players that the one to go over the finish line first, *without stepping on an egg*, will win for his team.

After the players are blindfolded, replace the eggs with many soda crackers. Place each cracker on a quarter of a sheet of newspaper. It's lots of fun for the spectators when a player steps on a soda cracker, supposing it is an egg. Players must walk and are not permitted to shuffle their feet. If a player succeeds in crossing the finish line without stepping on a cracker, he wins for his team.

Award the winning team 5 points.

NOTE TO THE LEADER

Using the newspaper makes this contest an indoor or an outdoor idea. After the contest just wrap the broken crackers in the newspaper and discard.

7 relaxer activities

There comes a time in every party when the guests need a breathing spell. Keep teen-agers busy, but do not exhaust them. Every program must have an intermission, but plan it carefully. Never call an intermission until you are sure you have captured the interest of the group sufficiently so that they will be eager to return to the activity afterwards. Intermissions should not be prolonged but should give the older teen-agers time to mingle and "chat." Intermissions for young teen-agers should be short. The activity following an intermission should be something spirited. It is almost like starting the party again. Everyone's interest must again be recaptured.

No two groups of teen-agers will react to the same activity in the same way. An activity one group enjoyed very much might fall flat with the next group. A leader will often find himself switching to an activity entirely different from the one he had planned because it seems to suit the group better. The success or failure of a game or activity depends greatly upon the way it is introduced by the leader. One of the biggest factors that help to determine the success of a party hostess's program is the enthusiasm the leader displays. Enthusiasm is contagious, and teen-agers are quick to sense the attitude of the youth leader. The satisfaction and pleasure the teen-ager receives from an activity is measurable only by the amount of enthusiasm he feels and expresses. Youth leaders must be the masters of the situations in which they find themselves. Self-confidence leads to successful achievement.

There comes a "psychological moment" in every party when one more game or one more dance might spoil the happy, joyous feeling that has been so prevalent all evening. If the group is made up of older teen-agers and you sense this, start rounding off the program, even though the program will not last as long as was planned. Send the guests home while they are still laughing.

The following are good games to use when you, as a youth leader, sense that the cadence of the party should be changed.

personal treasure hunt

NUMBER OF PLAYERS—Ten boys and ten girls plus any number of additional players.

MATERIALS NEEDED—A pencil and a Personal Treasure Hunt sheet for each player (see sample sheet).

This is an entertaining diversion the teen-agers will thoroughly enjoy. They'll need clear vision and quick power of observation.

During an intermission the leader, quietly and unseen by the others, gives one of the following twenty written instructions to ten boys and ten girls. Each of the chosen ten boys and ten girls complies with the particular instruction that he or she has received. The leader allows about five minutes for the boys to get ready for the

INSTRUCTIONS FOR BOYS

(1)

Put a comb in your hip pocket.

(2)

Ask the leader for a rubber band. Use it as a garter.

(3)

Turn your wrist watch so that you will be looking at it upside down.

(4)

Change your shoes so that they are on the wrong feet.

(5)

Trade one shoe with another guest so that you will both be wearing mismated shoes.

(6)

Ask the leader for a thumbtack. Put it on the sole of your shoe.

(7)

Ask the leader for two bobby pins. Conceal them in your hair.

(8)

Put a penny in the cuff of your trousers.

(9)

Lace one of your shoes from the top down.

(10)

Ask the leader for a Band-Aid. Put it on your right elbow.

PERSONAL TREASURE HUNT. The girls should be ready to do their part by the time the boys' part of the hunt is over.

All male players, including the ten boys with the special instructions, sit in a large circle. Each girl is given a pencil and a sheet marked "Personal Treasure Hunt for Girls" (see sample sheet on next page).

The object for the girls is to find the boys with the items listed on the treasure list. For example, each girl picks out a boy and has him stand; she searches him to find out whether or not he has a comb in his hip pocket. When she finds a treasure, she writes the boy's name in the proper blank, then goes on to search for the next item. When the girls have had ample time to search the boys, the leader asks all the guests to sit down and then says: "Will the boy with a comb in his hip pocket please stand." This boy's name is announced, and the girls check their own answers. The girl with the most correct list of names receives a prize.

The pencils and the "Personal Treasure Hunt for Boys" are distributed to the boys. All the girls, including the ten with the special assignments, sit down. The boys then hunt for the treasures on their lists. The boy with the most correct list of girls' names also receives a prize.

NOTE TO THE LEADER

If you noticed, some of the guests were instructed to ask you for certain small articles, so have them on hand:

Band-Aid	Paper Clip	Thumbtack
Rubber Band	Bobby Pins	Paper Bow

INSTRUCTIONS FOR GIRLS

(1) Wear just one earring.	(6) Put a penny in your shoe.
(2) Remove one stocking.	(7) Put some lipstick behind your right ear.
(3) Exchange one earring with another girl.	(8) Pin a paper bow to the back of your dress.
(4) Turn your wrist watch so that you will be looking at it upside down.	(9) Put your shoes on the wrong feet.
(5) Trade one shoe with another girl so that you both will be wearing mismated shoes.	(10) Ask the leader for a paper clip. Place it on the back of your collar.

(cut)

PERSONAL TREASURE HUNT FOR GIRLS

Search the boys. Find the ones with the treasures. Write their names on the lines.

(1) ______________________
(Comb in hip pocket)

(2) ______________________
(Rubber band on sock)

(3) ______________________
(Watch on upside down)

(4) ______________________
(Shoes on wrong feet)

(5) __________&__________
(Wearing mismated shoes)

(6) ______________________
(Thumbtack on shoe sole)

(7) ______________________
(Bobby pins in hair)

(8) ______________________
(Penny in trouser cuff)

(9) ______________________
(Shoe laced from top)

(10) ______________________
(Band-Aid on elbow)

Keep this paper. The correct answers will be announced.

(Sample Sheet)

PERSONAL TREASURE HUNT FOR BOYS

Search the girls. Find the ones with the treasures. Write their names on the lines.

(1) ______________________
(Only one earring)

(2) ______________________
(Only one stocking)

(3) __________&__________
(Mismated earrings)

(4) ______________________
(Watch upside down)

(5) __________&__________
(Mismated shoes)

(6) ______________________
(A penny in shoe)

(7) ______________________
(Lipstick behind ear)

(8) ______________________
(Paper bow on dress)

(9) ______________________
(Shoes on wrong feet)

(10) ______________________
(Paper clip on collar)

Keep this paper. The correct answers will be announced.

barnyard peanut hunt

NUMBER OF PLAYERS—Any number, divided into three or more groups.

MATERIALS NEEDED—Peanuts in the shell; a paper bag for each group.

Peanuts or individually wrapped pieces of candy are hidden in various places around the room or playing area. The players are divided into three or more groups and stand together as teams in different sections of the room. One player from each group is selected to act as captain and is given a paper bag. Each group is given the name of an *animal* (dog, sheep, cow, pig, etc.). When assigning each group an animal's name, the leader asks the group to demonstrate the sound their animal makes. The object of the game is to see which team can collect the most peanuts.

The leader explains the following rules.

1. No one but the captain of each team can pick up the peanuts.
2. When a player locates a peanut, he stands over it, points, and gives his team's call. He continues to call and point to the peanut until his captain comes to pick it up. The player then continues to look for other peanuts.
3. The captain uses the paper bag to collect the peanuts.
4. If two players from opposite teams spy the same peanut, they both stand by it, point, and give their team call. The first captain to arrive and pick up the peanut is, of course, the owner.
5. On the signal "Go," the players scatter and start to look for peanuts.

When the leader halts the hunt, each team sits down together and the captain counts the peanuts. Those found by each team are divided equally among the players on the team.

NOTE TO THE LEADER

This game is excellent to use for picnic activity.

how about that?

NUMBER OF PLAYERS—Six to twenty five players.
MATERIALS NEEDED—None.

Since this is a parlor game, the players sit in any formation.

The leader and all the players, except one player who is asked to leave the room, know the secret of this game and are pledged to secrecy. While the player is out of the room, the group selects three objects in the room that are in plain sight—for example, a chair, rug, and lamp. By this prearrangement any player from this group who is asked to leave the room later on will know what object to mention when he returns. When the first player returns to the room, the leader explains to him that he is to pick up the *thoughts* of the other players and *name the object* they are all concentrating upon. The player who just returned to the room sits in a chair while the leader strokes his forehead and tells him to concentrate, then name the first object that comes into his mind.

Here's the trick: No matter what object he mentions, the leader and other players applaud him and marvel at his power of concentration, making believe that the object he mentioned was correct.

Another player is sent from the room. Now in the presence of the first player, the group decides that the next object they will concentrate upon will be the chair. (Of course the person who left the room knows this and will say, "chair," when he returns.) A second and third person are sent from the room. The second person will say on his return, "rug," and the third player will say, "lamp."

The first player just will not be able to understand how he was able to name the correct object. In fact, he may begin to think he has superhuman powers, and he'll still be wondering the next day unless someone tells him the secret.

pirate treasure hunt

NUMBER OF PLAYERS—Three couples and any number of spectators.

MATERIALS NEEDED—Two blindfolds and a table.

One boy is chosen as the pirate, and a girl is selected to be the "treasure." The leader places a blindfold on each player. The boy stands on one side of the table, and the girl stands at the opposite side. Both players place their hands on the table. When the leader signals "Go," the boy and girl begin to move around the table. The girl tries to stay away from the boy, while the boy tries to find her. Both move cautiously and quietly in order not to reveal their whereabouts. When the "bump" comes as a big surprise to both, the blindfolds are removed and a new couple takes their places.

When the third couple is busy chasing each other around the table, the leader quietly asks the girl to step away from her position around the table. The boy not knowing this will continue to hunt, much to the amusement of the other players.

market open

NUMBER OF PLAYERS—Seven up to thirty.
MATERIALS NEEDED—Seven cards for each person.

This game can be counted on to enliven any party.

Use uniform pieces of light cardboard on which to print the names of as many of the following fruits and vegetables as there are players in the game:

Apple
Apricot
Banana
Bean
Beet
Cantalope
Carrot
Celery
Cherry
Grape
GARLIC
Lemon
Lime
Olive
Onion
Orange
Parsnip
Pea
Pear
Peach
Pepper
Pineapple
Plum
Potato
Prune
Radish
Spinach
Turnip
Tomato
Watermelon

If there are seven players, the leader prepares seven cards bearing the word "Apple," seven cards labeled "Apricot," seven "Banana," and so on. No matter what other fruits or vegetables are chosen, be sure to include seven cards labeled "Garlic."

The leader gives each person seven cards that have been well shuffled, then announces, "Market Open!" By moving about and exchanging cards with each other, the players try to be first to get seven cards alike. As he moves around the room, the player calls, "one for one," "two for two," or, "three for three." This means he wishes to exchange that number of cards with someone else. When he finds another player who wishes to exchange the same number of cards, these two trade cards. A player continues trading until he has seven cards alike. The cards marked Garlic *do not count.* Players should trade these cards with someone else as soon as possible. The first person to collect seven cards that are alike is declared the winner.

NOTE TO THE LEADER

If there are twenty people present, be sure to use only the names of twenty vegetables or fruits when you shuffle the cards. Otherwise the game will be unbalanced. You may want to shuffle the cards before the guests arrive and secure each hand with a rubber band. This makes it easier to distribute the cards.

he-man checkers

NUMBER OF PLAYERS—Two teams, three girls and three boys plus a captain for each team.

MATERIALS NEEDED—Fourteen chairs.

There's lots of jumping around to do in this

contest, and it is a *real* challenge for the captains of the teams.

Place seven chairs back to back in two rows. The middle chair in each row is empty. Players from each team sit in this order: Three boys—vacant chair—three girls. The red team occupies one row of chairs and the blue team the other. A captain stands in back of each team.

The game is played like Checkers. The object is to get the boys over to where the girls are sitting and vice versa by moving or jumping *one chair at a time*. Players must not move unless directed by the captain. (Example: The captain taps a player on his team and says, "Move one chair to the right," or "Jump over this player," etc.) No player can move backwards. If the captain gets stuck, he may ask the players to start over again as many times as is necessary, or he may ask any guest from his team who is not in this particular contest to assist him. The red team competes against the blue team to see which can accomplish the feat first.

NOTE TO THE LEADER

The secret is to alternate the moving of the boys and girls in this order:

(1) Move girl (2) Jump boy (3) Move boy

Alternate the above.

(1) Move boy (2) Jump girl (3) Move girl

The third move is the important move and the *key* to the puzzle. Practice before trying this in public.

human scrabble

NUMBER OF PLAYERS—Two teams, with up to twenty players on each team.

MATERIALS NEEDED—The letters of the alphabet on individual cards.

Talk about being "crazy mixed up?" This'll do it!

Divide the players into two teams. Distribute a set of alphabetical cards printed in red ink to one team and a set of blue letters to the other team. These cards are pinned near each guest's left shoulder.

The members of each team search about for letter-bearers who, together with themselves, make up a word of three letters or more. When the word is established, the "living letters" join hands and rush to the judges' table. (The leader and an appointed player act as judges and are stationed at a designated place.) The judges write the word on a slip of paper and give credit to the team. If a word is repeated, it is not counted. As soon as credit has been given for the word, the letters separate and rush off to find other letters to make up another word.

NOTE TO THE LEADER

If the group is too small for teams, each *individual* member of a word receives credit when a group forming a word presents itself before the judges' table.

royal order of the hens

NUMBER OF PLAYERS—Any number.
MATERIALS NEEDED—Two hard-boiled eggs.

This may sound like a silly stunt, but don't forget that the silliest sounding games often turn out to be the most fun.

Before the stunt starts, the leader "briefs" one of the guests on the duties of Her Royal Highness. The leader gives this person two hard-boiled eggs and instructs her to keep them concealed until a signal is given to place them on the seat of the appointed player's chair.

Two chairs are placed in front of the audience, and two girls are asked to leave the room. The leader introduces the guest he has chosen to be Her Royal Highness, and she sits on one of the chairs. The rest of the audience is asked to co-operate by clapping, cheering, and giving the girls a "big build-up" when they return to the room. (The success of this stunt depends a great deal upon the enthusiasm of the leader and his ability to ad lib.)

One girl is asked to return to the room. She is escorted to the front of the room by the leader and introduced to the audience and to Her Royal Highness. *(Audience applauds.)*

LEADER. While you were out, we formed a club. We would be delighted to have you as a member. Would you like to join?

ANSWER. Yes. *(Audience applauds.)*

LEADER. The name of the club is The Royal Order of the Hens. Do you still want to join?

ANSWER. Yes. *(Audience applauds.)*

LEADER. You must first pass a test. Show us how a hen scratches in a barnyard.

PLAYER. Demonstrates how a hen scratches. *(Audience applauds.)*

LEADER. Now let us hear how a hen cackles.

PLAYER. Demonstrates how a hen cackles. *(Audience applauds.)*

LEADER. Now you are ready for your final test. Sit beside Her Royal Highness. Flap your wings and cackle like a hen for fifteen seconds.

PLAYER. Flaps her arms and cackles. *(Audience applauds.)*

LEADER. You did well. You are now a member of The Royal Order of Hens. Stand and bow to the audience. *(While she is bowing to the audience, Her Royal Highness places two hard-boiled eggs on the chair where she has been sitting.)*

LEADER. Now turn and bow to Her Royal Highness.

PLAYER. Turns and bows to Her Royal Highness and discovers she has *laid two eggs.* (Watch her expression!)

NOTE TO THE LEADER

Call the second girl into the room. Initiate her into the Royal Order of the Hens.

Stunts of this sort should be used only with groups where everyone feels secure and at home. They can be embarrassing if a sensitive person is chosen.

well-known sayings

NUMBER OF PLAYERS—Any number.
MATERIALS NEEDED—A card table, large piece of paper and a crayon.

Tape the large piece of paper to the top of the card table. Collapse the legs and place the card table on a chair, so that it can be readily seen by all the players.

The leader writes the first letters of any well-known saying, quotation, or proverb on the paper. The object is to see which person in the audience can be the first to recognize the quotation.
For example, A R S G N M (A rolling stone gathers no moss).

The person who is able to recognize and call out the most proverbs is declared the winner and receives a prize. Suggested quotations are the following:

A stitch in time saves nine.
A fool and his money soon part.
One good turn deserves another.
Look before you leap.
Strike while the iron is hot.
Do unto others as you would have others do unto you.
The early bird gets the worm.
An apple a day keeps the doctor away.

seat shifting

NUMBER OF PLAYERS—Ten to thirty per circle.
MATERIALS NEEDED—A chair for each player.

Players sit on the chairs arranged in a circle. One person is chosen to go to the center of the circle and be "It." This leaves a vacant chair in the circle. When all is ready, "It" says, "Everybody shift to the right." The person next to the vacant chair moves into it, and everyone else in the circle also moves. While everyone is shifting, "It" tries to get a seat. If he is not successful in getting a seat, he may call, "Everyone shift left." "It" will in time find a seat. The player left without a seat becomes the next "It."

rhythm

NUMBER OF PLAYERS—Fifteen to twenty players per circle.

MATERIALS NEEDED—Chalk or a numbered slip of paper for each chair.

Number each chair either by writing the number on the floor with chalk or by placing a numbered slip of paper on the floor in front of each chair. The space of about three chairs is left vacant in the circle. This space separates the head from the foot of the circle.

Players sit in consecutive order around the circle. The head player's number is one. The second person is two, and so on. The object of the game is for each player to try to advance to chair number *one* and hold this position as long as possible.

Player number one begins the game by starting the following motions in rhythm. All the players in the circle do the same motions in the same rhythm with player number one.

1st Count—Slap both knees.

2nd Count—Clap both hands.

3rd Count—Snap fingers on right hand. The player who is "It" calls his own number. For example, number one calls, "One."

4th Count—Snap fingers on left hand. The player

who is "It" calls someone else's number, for example, number one calls, "Six."

Number six is the next person to lead the group. He calls his own number on the third count and someone else's number on the fourth count.

This action continues until someone fails to respond instantly to the number of the chair on which he is sitting, or until another player responds out of turn. When this happens, the person making the error must move to the last chair in the circle, and those players who occupied the intervening chairs must move one chair toward the head of the circle. Each time a player moves, his number changes. When the players who were required to move have found their places, player number one starts the RHYTHM again.

number scramble

NUMBER OF PLAYERS—Up to twenty players per circle.
MATERIALS NEEDED—A chair for each player.

This NUMBER SCRAMBLE game is a lively pastime for those who enjoy fun and confusion.

The players sit in a circle with *one less chair* than there are players. The leader gives each player a consecutive number. A player is chosen to be "It," and he goes to the center of the circle. "It" calls two numbers. The persons whose numbers are called must change places. The player in the center tries to secure one of their chairs. The person left without a chair to sit on becomes the center player, or "It." He will call the next two numbers. Should the player in the center call, "Everybody change!" each person must change to another chair. The person without a chair after the scramble is the next "It."

pick 'em up

NUMBER OF PLAYERS—Six to eight players per card table.
MATERIALS NEEDED—As many card tables as needed; colored peanuts and toothpicks.

Six to eight boys and girls stand around a card table for this vicious game in which it's every man for himself.

Before the party the host colors a pound of peanuts in the shell by dipping them in food coloring. Most of the peanuts are red, a lesser number are yellow, and only a few are colored blue.

Mix the colored peanuts thoroughly and place them in a large bowl in the center of the card table. Give each player two toothpicks. On the signal "Go," players—all at the same time—reach into the bowl with their toothpicks, lift peanuts from the bowl and place them in an individual pile. Each player tries to get as many peanuts as he can. The color is important too. Red peanuts count 2 points, yellow ones count 5 points—but every blue peanut counts 10 points. It is not fair to use fingers at any time.

When all of the peanuts have been removed from the bowl, the players count their score. Award the player with the highest score a prize.

human tick-tack-toe

NUMBER OF PLAYERS—Two teams. Nine players on each team. As many sets of two teams as desired.
MATERIALS NEEDED—Chalk to draw a diagram, or nine pieces of paper.

Everyone has played the pencil and paper game called Tick-Tack-Toe.

The same game can be played by drawing the diagram (or placing nine pieces of newspaper) on the floor and using people to represent the X's and O's.

Divide the players into two teams. If it's a boy-girl party, it's fun to have the girls play against the boys. The first player walks to the diagram (or papers) and takes any position he desires, to represent an X. Then the first player from the opposite side takes his position, to represent an O.

X	O	X
O	O	X
O	X	X

The object of each team is to prevent the other team from getting *three players standing in a row.* The team that succeeds in getting three of their players standing in a row is the winner of the round. These players go back to their original places, and a new round is started.

Teams alternate in starting each round. Players may not change places once they have stepped into a spot. Keep score for each team.

spy the objects

NUMBER OF PLAYERS—Any number.
MATERIALS NEEDED—A pencil and an answer sheet for each guest; articles listed below (sample sheet on next page).

Give each person a list of ten objects which have been "hidden" but are still in *plain sight.* Players may search anywhere in the room. No object is covered up.

Each player, with his list in hand, starts search-

(Sample Sheet)

SPY THE OBJECTS

Look around the room for the objects listed below. They are in plain sight. Don't tell anyone when you spy one. After you have left the spot, write down where you saw it.

Look for:	Where did you see it?
Button	
Paper Clip	
Dollar Bill	
Rubber Band	
Postage Stamp	
Toothpick	
Shoestring	
Scotch Tape	
Thread	
Ring	

ing for the objects. If he spies one, he makes no outward signs that he has seen one of the objects. He takes a couple of steps in the opposite direction to throw the others off the trail and then writes on his paper where the object is hidden. The first person finding the entire list of objects wins.

The fun of this game for the leader is to blend the objects so well with the furnishings in the room that a person can be looking straight at the article and not see it, such as in the following examples:

Button	Find one that is the same color as the drapes and sew button to drape.
Paper Clip	Have a confederate ask for a glass of water. After a few sips, drop paper clip in the glass.
Dollar Bill	Fold it around the back of a book to cover the title. Place on shelf with other books.
Rubber Band	Place it around the leg of a chair.
Postage Stamp	Take stamp off an old envelope and paste on the cover of a magazine of similar color.
Toothpick	Carefully place it in the soil of a flower pot.
Shoestring	Make it look like part of a picture frame.
Scotch Tape	Use the transparent kind and place about a four-inch strip on a glass surface.
Yarn	Choose a color nearly matching the color of a lamp shade. Make it look like part of the shade.
Bracelet or Ring	Place around control buttons on television set.

8 games for any time

Every leader or parent needs some tricks up his or her sleeve. They come in handy for early arrivals, the late-stayers, the club, the impromptu gathering, and other occasions when casual entertainment is what a group wants.

These are not necessarily party activities. Some of them can be used on trips or on rainy days, around a campfire or around the kitchen table. Some are fine for dinners or banquets. All of them have a party flavor because they're fun. And so they've been included—just for fun!

out you go

This is a fun-filled game for a small group who are just sitting around.

Have several large pieces of paper taped to the wall. Think of some easy slogans or phrases, such as "Three Blind Mice," "Roses are Red," "Time to Retire." Use one large piece of paper for each slogan or phrase and make a series of dashes, one dash for each letter in each word. Here is an example of a phrase:

T - - -
T -
- - T - - -

When playing starts, the leader gives the group a hint. In the example above, the dashes stand for "Time to Retire." The hint might be: "Something you do when you get sleepy." Each player, in turn, calls out a letter he thinks will fill in the words. If a player calls out, "L," for example, the leader says, "Out you go!" There is no "L" in the words, so that player is out. If someone says, "I," you fill in every "I" in the phrase.

The person who first recognizes the phrase is the winner.

pass the scissors

This game is old stuff perhaps, but it's fun. Guests sit in a circle or informally around the room.

The game starts with the first person saying, "I'm going to pass the scissors crossed or uncrossed. Watch very carefully, for you must pass them on to the next person exactly as I have passed them to you." The passer makes much to-do about opening and closing the scissors. After fussing with them, trying to confuse the receiver, he passes on the scissors either open or shut. The passer says, "I pass them to you crossed (or uncrossed)." The trick is that the words "crossed" and "uncrossed" do not refer to the position of the scissor blades, but to the position of the passer's feet.

One by one the players catch on. But with the right footwork, they continue to baffle the guests who have not been so observant.

mind reading

The mind reader leaves the room. The leader asks the group to select a thing or person anywhere in the world. Let's say the group has selected a bicycle. The mind reader returns to the room. The leader asks him questions such as, "Is it this vase?" ("No"); "Is it a dog?" ("No"); Is it an automobile?" ("No"); "Is it a bicycle?" ("Yes").

How did the mind reader know? He and the leader had agreed upon a signal. When the leader used the signal, the mind reader knew that the next question was It. In this case, the signal was "anything with wheels." An automobile has wheels, so the mind reader answered "yes" to the next question. The leader will not use "automobile" twice; he'll use "wagon," "train," or other things that have wheels.

The next signal might be the colors in the American flag. The leader could ask, "Is it Marge's dress?" (red) or "Bill's shirt" (white) or "this dish?" (blue). On the very next question after naming something red, white, or blue, he names It. The mind reader says, "yes," and the group is amazed at his talent.

cutting up

A pair of scissors and a stack of old magazines will be needed. Make up a list of articles that are to be hunted by going through the magazines. Set a time limit, because racing to win is more than half the excitement. Explain that the cutting should be done as neatly as possible.

Give each guest a list of pictures to be found.

The list might be something like this:

Car	Silverware	Dog
Man	Telephone	Pipe
Lady	Umbrella	Toothbrush
Boy	Eyeglasses	Book
Girl	House	Tree

If there are boys and girls, let them draw for partners and play as couples. Here is an important rule: Permit only one magazine to be used at a time by a couple. A prize is awarded to the couple who find all the pictures, or have found the most when time is up.

target practice

This is fun for a crowd spending a quiet evening together.

Give each person a drinking straw and five toothpicks of the kind that come in different colors. Each person receives five toothpicks of the same color. See who can blow his toothpick the furthest. Each person, in turn, puts toothpick in straw and straw in mouth, and then blows.

Next set up a target. Put a large bowl in the center of the coffee table and see who can land the most toothpicks in the bowl. Later make the target smaller. Place a glass or Jane's shoe on the table and see who can score the most hits.

toothpick pick up

Dump a box of toothpicks in the center of the table. Give each teen-ager seated around it two toothpicks to use as tongs. Each, in rotation, gets a turn at lifting picks from the pile, using his tongs. If a player drops or even jars one in the dump, he must return to the pile the toothpick he was lifting and forfeit his turn.

The player finishing with the most toothpicks is the winner.

ghosts

GHOSTS is fun because of its amusing rules.

Everyone sits around in a circle or informally. The first player starts the game by saying, "I'm thinking of a word that starts with C." The next player must add another letter to help form a word beginning with C. Everyone in the group adds a letter until someone is forced to end the word. The next person starts another word, and the game goes on.

Here are the rules: The player who ended the first word becomes a half-ghost, and it's against the rules to talk to him. Anyone who does is a half-ghost too. Half-ghosts try to trick the other players into talking to them. If a half-ghost ends another word (his second), he becomes a full ghost and is out of the game.

If anyone adds a letter that does not belong in any word, a player may challenge that player's word. If he has been bluffing (or misspelling), he becomes a half-ghost. If he has a proper word, the challenger becomes a half-ghost. The game goes on until everyone except one (the winner) is a full ghost.

common delusion

One player, "It," leaves the room. The rest of the group decide on a COMMON DELUSION under which they are suffering. If it's Halloween, they may decide they're a witch, cat, pumpkin, or owl. At some other party maybe the delusion (or dreaming) is a famous person—John D. Rockefeller, the President, or a local celebrity such as the principal of their school, the history teacher, or the football coach. Then again it might be the performance of some feat, like orbiting the earth or crawling through a jungle.

When "It" returns, everyone in the room must make proper gestures and motions to suit the delusion that was chosen. "It" has three chances to give the correct answer. If "It" guesses correctly, he chooses someone else to take his place. If after three guesses "It" does not give the correct answer, the leader chooses another player to leave the room.

think of a song

Everyone sits in a circle. The object of the game is to think of as many songs as possible that mention a girl's name. The first person starts singing a song such as "Hello Dolly," "Marie," or "Once in Love With Amy." The other guests join in the singing. (If all of the words cannot be recalled, just hum the tune.) The second person starts another song, and so on. If a player cannot think of a song, he forfeits his turn but is still eligible to sing with the group. The game continues until everyone but one person has forfeited his turn. That player is declared the winner.

Next use the names of states, cities, or boys.

gossip

This is a funny game that shows how easily the truth can be twisted.

The group is sitting around in a circle when the first person, starting the game, softly whispers to his neighbor a rather long made-up remark, such as, "Did you hear about Mary Brown and Susie Smith taking their dogs to the vets the other day for shots?" The receiver of the news repeats the remark in a soft whisper in the ear of his closest neighbor. The message circulates the room. The last person to hear the message stands and tells aloud what he's heard. Ten chances to one he heard that both Mary and Susie got shot.

To make this game effective, there should be at least ten to twenty players.

follow directions

Giving this test to a group of people provides a lot of fun. The object is to see how carefully they read directions and follow instructions. The number of people who skip details when reading is amazing!

Give each guest a pencil, and place the following test *face down* on the table in front of him. This paper must not be turned over until the leader gives the signal to start. The leader announces: "This is a two-minute test. Complete it as quickly as you can. Turn your paper over and start." (Sample of the test is on the next page.)

NOTE TO THE LEADER

The real humor of this test comes when people discover they have gone through all these contortions *unnecessarily*. Had they followed the directions and read

(Sample Test)

O ________________________

TIMED TEST IN FOLLOWING DIRECTIONS

1. Read everything before you do anything.
2. Write your name on the line at the top of the page.
3. Circle the word "top" in sentence number two.
4. Shade the circle at the top of the page.
5. Multiply: 522 × 2
6. Push your chair back. Stand up, turn around once, then sit down again.
7. Write the word "hurry" backwards. (_ _ _ _ _)
8. Make a fist. Pound on the table *three* times.
9. Tap your nearest neighbor on the shoulder and say: "Hi, my directions say I am to do this. I'll talk with you later."
10. Remove one shoe. Wave it over your head three times.
11. Stand up. Bow to the person on your right then to the person on your left. Sit down again.
12. Clap your hands and bounce on the seat three times.
13. Stand up. Wave your right hand over your head and shout "Whoopee." Sit down.
14. Underline sentence Number One.
15. Now that you have finished reading everything carefully, do only what you are asked to do in sentence Number Two.

the entire test, as instructed to do in sentence number one, they would have discovered in sentence number fifteen that they were asked merely to write their name at the top of the page.

It's kind of a silly test, but everybody has fun.

whistle

Two to six players sit around a table. A deck of cards is placed face down on the table in front of each player. One player gives the signal to "Go," then all turn up one card simultaneously from their own deck. The cards must be turned up slowly toward the center of the table. It is not fair for a player to turn the cards toward himself! The players must keep their eyes open for Kings, Queens, and Jacks. When two players turn up Kings, each must quickly say a boy's name. When two Queens appear at the same time, each player must call out a girl's name. When two Jacks are turned up at the same time, each player must *whistle*. No name may be used more than once in any one round. The player calling out first and correctly gives all his upturned cards to the slower player. The one who gets rid of all his cards first is the winner.

NOTE TO THE LEADER

Instead of using a complete deck of cards for each person, you can distribute the cards equally among the players.

character reading

Surprise your group by reading their characters in this nutty way.

While sitting around a room or around a table at some church or school affair, pass a bowl of walnuts and ask each person to take one. They all crack them open and are surprised to find a silly character reading inside. Have each person stand, in turn, and read what was said about his character to the group, then tell why he thinks this statement about him is true.

Here are some suggestions to write on individual slips of paper:

A leader, executive type
Has initiative and self-confidence
A tender, gentle type
Creative, companionable, and peace-loving
Social type
Lots of personality
Fine, steady type
Orderly, methodical mind
Good judgment
Independent type
Loves new faces, new places, new ideas
Loves people more than anything
The rough and ready type
The poetic, mysterious type
Imaginative type
Money-making type
Forceful, courageous type
Powerful and tactful type
The fearless type
A leader in noble causes
Unselfish type
Sympathetic type
Broadminded and understanding

NOTE TO THE LEADER

Before the party, split the walnuts in two, remove the nut meat, put the slips of paper in the shell, then glue or scotch-tape the halves of the nuts together.

dig deeper

The surprise ending of this stunt never fails to amuse the group.

Some type of music or a whistle is essential for this stunt. Everyone sits around in a circle or around a table. Clean tin cans are distributed so that every fifth or sixth person is holding a can in his hand. The leader announces: "The committee wishes to raise some money, and we are asking for your help. Please take a penny from your pocket or purse."

The leader waits until everyone has found a penny. When the music starts, those with the cans pass them to the person on their right. Each person receiving a can passes it on until the music stops. The persons who have cans in their possession when the music stops, must pay a penalty. The penalty applies only to those who are holding the can when the music stopped. If two people are touching the some can, both will pay a penalty. The players who were caught, must forfeit a penny and drop it in the can. After the penalties are paid, the music starts again.

After a few rounds at a penny, the leader raises the price of the penalty to five cents. He waits until each person finds or borrows a nickel. The climax of the game occurs when the prices is raised to ten cents. There will be real enthusiasm now. Everyone, in view of what he thinks is going to happen will be very, very, anxious to pass the can along to the next person as quickly as possible. When the music stops this time, every person who has a can in his possession is asked to stand and deposit his dime in the can. The leader then announces: "You folks are the *winners*. All of the money in the can belongs to you!"

NOTE TO THE LEADER

Older teen-agers enjoy this game. It is a good stunt to use between courses if they are attending a youth dinner.

For younger teens who do not have nickels and dimes in their pockets, start the game by giving each guest six or seven pieces of paper wrapped candy. The winners may keep the candy that is in the can.

✓ chug-a-lug

This is a memory and co-ordination test that will really keep the group alert.

Supply each person with a glassful of some kind of beverage. The group sits around a table. The leader starts by announcing that he wishes to drink a toast to everyone present. He asks everyone to follow his speech and actions with the greatest concentration, so that they will be able in turn to propose the same toast after him. Each performs with the leader, doing everything the same as he does.

The following routine must be done in this *exact* order:

1. Stand. Hold the glass between the thumb and first finger of your right hand. Raise the glass in salute and say, "Here's to your health for the first time."
2. Take one sip from the glass.
3. Sit down and bounce on the chair once.
4. Tap the glass on the table once.
5. Rub the back of your right hand over your lips once.
6. Rub the back of your left hand over your lips once.

7. Tap the top of the table with the pointer finger of your right hand once.
8. Tap the top of the table with the pointer finger of your left hand once.
9. Tap the underside of the table with the pointer finger of your right hand.
10. Tap the underside of the table with the pointer finger of your left hand.
11. Slap your right knee with your right hand once.
12. Slap your left knee with your left hand once.
13. Stamp your right foot on the floor once.
14. Stamp your left foot on the floor once.
15. Stand up and then sit down once.
16. Hold the glass in salute with the thumb and first finger of the right hand and say, "That was a toast to your health for the first time."
17. Everyone takes one sip from his glass.

The leader repeats the toast. He starts off by saying: "Here's to your health for the *second* time." In round two everything must be done *twice* (use two fingers with thumb to hold the glass, tap the glass on the table twice, stamp foot twice, etc.) In the next round everything is done *three* times.

The leader then turns to a person in the group and says, "Now let's see you lead the toast to our health." This person takes over and leads the group. He must follow the routine as demonstrated *exactly*. If he makes a mistake, everyone in the group calls out, "CHUG-A-LUG." He is disqualified and must drink the entire contents of his glass. When it is his turn again, he must start at the beginning regardless of the number of rounds he had previously completed successfully.

Each person takes his turn at proposing a toast. The one who can lead the group through the largest number of toasts, without a mistake, is declared the winner.

NOTE TO THE LEADER

Place a pitcherful of the beverage on the table, so that the glasses can be re-filled.

TRICKS

(Tricks are always fun. Following are a few your group may enjoy.)

turn the glasses over

Here's one for the crowd to try.

Place three empty glasses on the table in front of several players. The two end glasses are upside down, and the glass in the center is in an upright position.

The challenge is to get all three glasses into a right-side-up position in exactly three moves. Each move consists of turning over any two glasses at the same time. Two glasses (no more or less) must be turned over at each move. Can you do it? Give it a try.

NOTE TO THE LEADER

Practice this before you try it in public.

1. Reverse the position of second and third glasses.
2. Reverse the position of first and third glasses.
3. Reverse the position of second and third glasses.

snap it off

Here's a sleight-of-hand trick your crowd will enjoy trying.

Give a player a smooth card about the size of a playing card and a penny. He balances the card on the end of his left forefinger and places the penny on top of the card. With the middle finger of his other hand, he tries to snap off the card but keep the penny on his finger.

It sounds impossible, but it can be done. A penny is easier than a nickel. Try it with a nickel.

easy does it!

This amusing pastime is very simple but lots of fun and entertaining to people sitting around a table.

Place a bottle in the center of the table and give each contestant twenty kitchen matches. Each player takes a turn placing the matches, one at a time, on the top of a narrow-necked bottle. If a player knocks any matches off the bottle, he loses his turn and adds the fallen matches to his own supply.

The first player to get rid of his supply of matches is declared the winner and is awarded a prize. It is quite surprising how high a structure can be built in this manner. Give it a try.

nosie

Have someone in the group sit in a chair and lean his head back as far as possible. He must keep his head in this position. Now place a penny on the end of his nose. The trick for him is to wiggle his nose until the penny drops.

He surely makes some funny faces. Have someone else try it.

toothpick star

If your crowd likes to do tricks, try this.

Break five wooden toothpicks in half and place them on a saucer with the broken ends all together. Put two drops of water in the center of the broken ends. Surprise! The water causes the wood to expand, and the toothpicks move to form a perfect five-pointed star.

tongue twisters

Repeat the following sentences three times as rapidly as you can:

Round and round the rugged rocks the ragged rascal ran.

She's so selfish she should sell shellfish, but shellfish shells seldom sell.

Betty Blue blows big beautiful bubbles.

Two toads totally tired tried to trot to Tedbury.

Mitzi misses Miss Smith—Miss Smith misses Mitzi.

A crop of poppies in a copper coffee pot.

Seven slick slimy snakes sliding slowly southward.

Peter Pepper picked a peck of pickled peppers. A peck of peppers Peter Pepper picked. If Peter Pepper picked a peck of pickled peppers, where's the peck of pickled peppers Peter Pepper picked?

Bill Bore had a board bill and a billboard. Both the board bill and the billboard bored Bill Bore. So Bill Bore sold the billboard to pay the board bill and now neither the board bill nor the billboard will bore Bill Bore.

Betty Botta bought a bit o' butter. "But," said she, "this butter's bitter. If I put this butter in my batter, it will make my batter bitter." So Betty Botta bought a bit o' better butter and put it in her bitter batter, which made Betty Botta's bitter batter a bit better.

Terry Thistle is a successful thistle sifter. He sifts sieves full of three thousand thistles through the thick of his thumb. If those thistle sifters who sift sieves of thistles think of Terry Thistle the successful thistle sifter, they will be successful at sifting thistles through sieves too.

Mr. Shott and Mr. Nott agreed to fight a duel. Nott was shot and Shott was not, so it is better to be Shott than Nott. Shott and not Nott shot the shot that shot Nott. If the shot that Shott shot which shot Nott had shot Shott and not Nott, Shott instead of Nott would have been shot and Nott would not.

riddles

(answers on pages 116 to 118)

1. Take two letters from a five-letter word and have one left.
2. When has a farmer the best chance to see his pigs?
3. When is the only time a man is really immersed in his business?
4. What lives in winter and dies in summer?

5. What men are the most above board?
6. What contains more feet in winter than in summer?
7. What is the surest way to keep the water from coming into your house?
8. A man bought two fishes and had three when he got home. Explain this.
9. On which side of church does a cypress tree grow?
10. Why is the letter A like honeysuckle?
11. Why is O the noisiest vowel?
12. Why does a blow leave a blue mark when it is over?
13. What does a girl look for that she doesn't want to find?
14. What relation is the doormat to the doorstep?
15. What will be yesterday and was tomorrow?
16. What gets bigger the more you contract it?
17. When is onion soup sure to run out of the soup plates?
18. What kind of hen lays the longest?
19. When can a man be said to be head over ears in debt?
20. What is the difference between 16 ounces of lead and a pianist?
21. Why is handwriting in ink like a dead pig?
22. Why is the letter D like a bad boy?
23. Why is the letter E always grouchy?
24. What is the difference between a well-dressed man and a tired dog?
25. When is a soldier charitable?
26. What is the difference between a jeweler and a jailer?
27. What occurs once in a minute, twice in a moment, and not once in a hundred thousand years?
28. It belongs to you. Yet your friends, without buying, borrowing or stealing it, use it much more than you do. What is it?
29. Why can't we fight with actresses?
30. What is it that man wants yet no man wants to lose?

31. Where are you sure to go when you are twelve years old?
32. Which is correct: The white of the egg is yellow, or the white of the eggs are yellow?
33. Which candle burns longer: wax candles or tallow candles?
34. What speaks every language?
35. Why can't it rain for two days continually?
36. If eight sparrows are on a roof and you shoot one, how many remain?
37. How can five people divide five cookies so that each gets a cookie and yet one cookie remains on the plate?
38. What question can never be answered by "yes?"
39. What is full of holes yet holds water?
40. Four fat women under one small umbrella in a terrible storm. Why did they not get wet?
41. What is Walker's choice?
42. What is the only thing you break when you say its name?
43. What is bought by the yard yet worn by the feet?
44. What horse sees as much in the rear as he does in the front?
45. What's the best way to carry water in a sieve?
46. If a telephone and a piece of paper had a race, who would win?
47. Why is a man who doesn't go to the races and bet just as bad as one who does?
48. Why is the nose in the middle of the face?
49. In a certain word L is in the middle, in the beginning, and at the end. There is only one L in the word. What is the word?
50. What will go up the chimney down but will not go down the chimney up?

51. What goes from New York to Chicago without moving an inch?
52. Why is a caterpillar like a hot biscuit?
53. What is the difference between an old penny and a new dime?
54. What is the difference between a cloud and a spanked boy?
55. Why is Ireland the wealthiest country?
56. What is the difference between a cat and a comma?
57. What is the longest word in the English language?
58. What is the difference between a bad boy and a postage stamp?
59. What goes up and down and up and down but never touches the sky or ground?
60. What table is completely without legs?
61. Why should fish be well educated?
62. What is filled every morning and emptied every night except once a year when it is filled at night and emptied in the morning?
63. What has teeth but cannot chew?

crazy bets

(answers on page 119)

1. I bet I can put myself through a keyhole!
2. I bet I can jump across the street!
3. I bet I have something outside that will go out when it comes in!
4. I bet I have more money in my pocket than you have, no matter how much you have!
5. I bet I have a piece of paper in my pocket with some handwriting on it that you will want to pay me 90¢ for!

6. I bet you use something every day that doesn't belong to you.
7. I bet I can write a much longer word than you can, no matter what word you write!
8. I bet you can't take off your coat alone.
9. I bet I can take four from four and leave eight!
10. I bet you can't answer four questions wrong!

test your reasoning

(answers on page 119)

1. If you went to bed at 8 o'clock at night and set the alarm to get up at 9:00 in the morning, how many hours sleep would this permit you to have?
2. Do they have a 4th of July in England?
3. How many birthdays does the average man have?
4. If you had only one match and entered a room in which there was a kerosene lamp, an oil heater and a wood-burning stove, which would you light first?
5. Why can't a man living in Winston-Salem, N.C., be buried west of the Mississippi River?
6. Some months have 30 days, some have 31. How many have 28 days?
7. If a doctor gave you two pills and told you to take one every half hour, how long would they last?
8. A man builds a house with four sides to it, and it is rectangular in shape. Each side has southern exposure. A big bear comes wandering by. What color is the bear?
9. How far can a dog run into the woods?
10. What four words appear on every denomination of U.S. coins?

11. What is the minimum number of active baseball players "on the field" during any part of an inning? How many outs in an inning?
12. I have in my hand two U.S. coins which total 55¢ in value. The first one is not a nickel. What are the two coins?
13. A farmer had 17 sheep, and all but nine died. How many did he have left?
14. Divide 30 by ½ and add 10. What is the answer?
15. Two men are playing checkers. They play five games, and each man wins the same number of games. How can you figure this?
16. Take two apples from three apples and what do you have?
17. An archaeologist claimed he found a coin dated 56 B.C. Do you believe him?
18. A woman gives a beggar 50¢. The woman is the beggar's sister, but the beggar is not the woman's brother.
19. How many animals of each species did Moses take aboard the ark with him?
20. Is it legal in Florida for a man to marry his widow's sister?

answers to riddles

1. Take s and t from stone and have one.
2. When he has a sty in his eye.
3. When he is giving a swimming lesson.
4. An icicle.
5. Chessmen.

6. An outdoor skating rink.
7. Don't pay the water bill.
8. He had two fish–and one smelt.
9. The outside.
10. A *B* always follows it.
11. All the other vowels are in audible.
12. Because the past part of blow is blew.
13. A run in her stocking.
14. Step father.
15. Today.
16. Debts.
17. When there's a leek in it.
18. A dead one.
19. When he hasn't paid for the wig he's wearing.
20. The pianist pounds away and the lead weighs a pound.
21. Because it is done with a pen.
22. Because it makes ma mad.
23. Because, while it is never out of health or pocket, it never appears in good spirits.
24. The man wears an entire suit while the tired dog just pants.
25. When he presents arms.
26. One sells watches and the other watches cells.
27. The letter m.
28. Your name.
29. They make up too quickly.
30. A bald head.
31. Into your thirteenth year.
32. Neither. White is never yellow.
33. Neither. They both burn shorter.
34. An echo.
35. Because there is always a night between.
36. None. They all fly away.

37. The last person takes the plate with the cookie.
38. "Are you asleep."
39. A sponge.
40. It was a sand storm.
41. Mrs. Walker.
42. Silence.
43. Carpet.
44. A blind horse.
45. Freeze the water first.
46. The telephone, since the paper will always remain stationery.
47. Because he is no bettor.
48. Because it is a scenter.
49. The word is inland. L is in the middle. In is at the beginning. And is at the end.
50. An umbrella.
51. The road.
52. Because it makes the butterfly.
53. Nine cents.
54. A cloud pours with rain and a spanked boy roars with pain.
55. Because its capital is always Dublin.
56. A cat has claws at the end of paws; the comma has a pause at the end of a clause.
57. Smiles. There is a mile betwen the first and last letter.
58. One you lick with a stick and the other you stick with a lick.
59. A pump handle.
60. A timetable.
61. They are found in schools.
62. A stocking.
63. A comb.

answers for crazy bets

1. Write "myself" on a piece of paper and put it through the keyhole.
2. Go across the street and then jump.
3. Bring in a burning flashlight and turn it off as you come in.
4. Sure you have, since *his* money is not in your pocket.
5. Take out a dollar bill and show the signature of the Treasurer.
6. The alphabet or numbers.
7. Write "a much longer word than you can."
8. As soon as he does this, start to take your coat off too.
9. Take a square piece of paper and tear off the four corners. You end up with eight corners.
10. Ask three questions which he will answer wrong, then pause and say in an off-hand manner, "Let's see, that's three isn't it?" He will say *yes*, which is a *correct* answer.

answers to test your reasoning

1. One. The clock doesn't know you want to get up in the morning.
2. Yes. The calendar does not go from the 3rd to the 5th.
3. One. We are born only once. The rest are anniversaries.
4. Light the match first.
5. Because living people are not buried.

6. All months have 28 days. Some months have more than 28 days.
7. One-half hour. Take the first at 9 A.M. and the second at 9:30 A.M.
8. White. A house with four sides having southern exposures would have to be located at the North Pole. Polar bears are found at the North Pole. Polar bears are white.
9. Half-way. After he passes the half-way mark, he is on his way out.
10. United States of America.
11. Ten. Nine players plus one batter. Six. Three outs for each team.
12. A 50¢ piece and a nickel. The first coin is a 50¢ piece.
13. Nine. All but nine died.
14. 70. $30 \div \frac{1}{2} = \frac{30}{1} \times \frac{2}{1} = 60 + 10 = 70$
15. They were not playing each other.
16. Two apples. You took two.
17. No. The coin could not have been dated according to Christ's birth before the date of it was known.
18. It's not her brother. The beggar is her sister.
19. None. Noah took the animals aboard the ark.
20. His wife cannot be a widow if he is still living.

9 music and dance games

Using games that require musical background can add so very much to a teen-age social program. Music automatically lifts spirits, creates interest and gaiety, brings out the vivacity in people, and builds up the spontaneity which is the ultimate aim of any youth leader, parent, or party hostess.

chinese puzzle

NUMBER OF PLAYERS—Ten to forty players per circle.
MATERIALS NEEDED—Background music if desired.

This puzzle is for a group of good-natured, fun-loving teen-agers. It is not nearly so difficult to conduct as it is to describe, and it is an enjoyable experiment.

From ten to forty boys and girls join hands and stand in one large circle. The leader takes his place between two players in the circle and joins hands with them.

The leader, by maneuvering as described in the following paragraphs, literally *ties the circle in knots.* The object of the game is to get the circle *untangled* without anyone letting go of hands. It can be done!

The leader walks across the circle and ducks *under* the joined hands of two players. This will require everyone in the circle to move. All players follow the path set by the leader. Everyone follows exactly the same path as the person ahead of him. *Do not run.* The leader *slowly* weaves in and out, moving under the joined hands of the players in the circle. As a result of this weaving action, many players' arms will be crossed and their handclasps twisted. *Players must not let go of hands.*

After a short while, the leader stops his weaving in and out and leads the group into one large circle again. It may take a few seconds for the players at the opposite side of the circle to unwind. When all the twists have been untangled, the players will be standing in one large circle and the CHINESE PUZZLE will have been solved.

NOTE TO THE LEADER

Emphasize these three rules to the participants:

1. Do not let go of the persons' hands you are holding.
2. Do not run.
3. Follow the person in front of you.

Should the players be standing with their backs toward the center of the ring when you form the last circle, their positions can be righted if you *walk backwards* under the joined hands of one couple.

pass it along

NUMBER OF PLAYERS—Any number.
MATERIALS NEEDED—One paper swatter for every fifth or eighth person; music.

To make swatters, roll four double sheets of newspaper together. Tape to keep them from unrolling.

Players sit in a circle. The leader distributes the

swatters to the players by handing a swatter to every fifth or eighth player. The music starts, and the players with the swatters pass the swatters to the person on their *right*. Players continue to pass the swatters around the circle until the music stops unexpectedly.

A player who is in possession of a swatter when the music stops must *pay a penalty*. Each time he receives a swatter in the next round, he must pass it under his left knee. Every time the same player is caught holding a swatter when the music stops, a new and more serious penalty is added. For example, the *second* time he is caught he must pass the swatter under both knees. His *third* penalty will require him to stand up, sit down, and then pass the swatter. The *fourth* time he is caught he will stand up, turn completely around, sit down, and pass the swatter. Each time he is caught after this he adds one more turn before he sits down.

Award the person caught the most number of times a "booby" prize.

have a seat

NUMBER OF PLAYERS—Even number of girls and boys, plus one extra girl.

MATERIALS NEEDED—A chair for each boy.

This is a couple game and a version of Musical Chairs. It is a good pastime for dispelling any feeling of social inadequacy or shyness your guests might have. The object of the game is for each girl to find a *boy's lap* to sit on.

Provide a chair for each boy. Place the chairs in a line, alternating the seats so that every other chair is facing in the same direction. The boys sit on the chairs, and when the music starts the girls march around the boys. Be sure that there is one extra girl in line. When the music stops, each girl scrambles to find a boy's lap to sit on. The girl who does not find a seat is *out*. The leader removes the end chair from the line, and the boy who was occupying this chair must also leave the game. The music is started again, and the game continues until only one boy and one girl are left in the game. The girl is declared the winner and is awarded a prize.

NOTE TO THE LEADER

If chairs are not available, have the boys stand in a straight line facing in alternate directions. When the music starts, every boy kneels on one knee. This provides a lap for the girl to sit on.

Stop the music without warning.

who's doing it?

NUMBER OF PLAYERS—Any number.
MATERIALS NEEDED—None.

Players sit in a large circle. One player is asked to leave the room. The leader appoints one player in the circle to be "It." "It" is instructed to clap hands, tap feet, snap fingers, wave arms, make funny faces, etc., to the rhythm of music. The other players sitting in the circle are instructed to *mimic* the motions and actions of the person who is "It."

When the person who left the room returns, he is given three chances to name the person who is "It." If he guesses correctly, another player is selected to leave the room, and the leader appoints another player to be "It." "It" must be careful to change his action only when the person in the center is not looking in his direction.

NOTE TO THE LEADER

To end the game, send a player from the room. Tell the players sitting in the circle to make up their own individual motions. Naturally everyone will be doing something different. Needless to say, the player who returns to the room will be quite confused until he realizes what is happening.

For a more active game, have the players *stand* in a circle or *march* instead of sitting in a circle.

hats off to you!

NUMBER OF PLAYERS—As many as the leader can provide old hats for—plus one extra player.
MATERIALS NEEDED—Old hats.

This won't do anything for the girls' fancy hair styles, so you may prefer to try this with some of the boys, who will not have anything to complain about.

The players stand in a circle, and the leader gives each person, except one, an old hat. Each contestant places the hat on his head.

Music with an appropriate beat is played, or the leader counts as the contestants *exchange hats in rhythm*. On each count each player is instructed to remove the hat from his own head and place it on his neighbor's head. The leader will intermittently change the direction he is to pass, by calling out, "Change, pass to the *right*," or, "Change, pass to the *left*." When the music suddenly stops or the leader gives the command "Halt," the contestants stop passing. Any player who is without a hat, or in his confusion has passed his hat the wrong way, or is on the floor trying to recover a hat he has dropped, is eliminated and leaves the circle. The music or count is started again, and the game continues. The fun begins when the cadence is speeded up.

The last person standing in the circle and *still hatted* is declared the winner and receives a prize.

limbo

NUMBER OF PLAYERS—Any number.
MATERIALS NEEDED—Jump standards (or improvise by using piles of books on chairs); a Limbo record.

The players must really "bend over backwards" to win this contest.

The leader sets up the standards. A light pole is placed between the two posts. Adjust the pole so that it will fall easily if brushed against by a player. If you desire, two players can hold the pole. However, there is a chance of variation in the height if you do this.

Dancers line up individually, one behind the other, and take turns going under the horizontal bar. The bar is lowered after each person has gone under it or attempted to go under it. A dancer approaches the bar holding his chest high, head tilted straight back, feet spread apart, and arms extended out to the side. He bends backward as far as possible and with short, choppy steps in rhythm to the music goes under the bar. Dancers who (1) lose balance, (2) fail to keep head tilted back, (3) fall forward on knees, or (4) disturb the bar while attempting to go under it, are eliminated after three tries.

going to the dogs

NUMBER OF PLAYERS—Any number.
MATERIALS NEEDED—One paper swatter for every fifth or sixth person. Music.

To make swatter, roll four double sheets of newspaper together. Tape to keep them from unrolling.

Players sit in a circle. The leader distributes the paper swatters to the players by handing a swatter to every fifth or sixth person.

The music starts, and the players with the swatters pass the swatter to the person on their right. Players continue to pass the swatters around the circle until the music unexpectedly stops. A player who is in possession of a swatter when the music stops becomes a dog and must pay a penalty. Once he becomes a dog, he is a dog for the rest of the game. Each time he receives a swatter in the next round, he must stand and bark like a dog and sit down, then pass the swatter on to the person on his right. Every time the same player is caught holding the swatter when the music stops, he stands and adds one more bark, as an additional penalty—a person caught four times will stand and bark *four times* before he sits down and passes the swatter on.

When most of the players have gone to the dogs and it is almost impossible to hear the music, award the person caught the most times a box of dog biscuits as a "booby" prize.

how low can you go?

NUMBER OF PLAYERS—Any number, in couples or as individuals.

MATERIALS NEEDED—A light pole 6 to 8 feet long; jumping standards or two piles of books.

Crawling around on all fours is just what is expected of the players in this contest. Teen-agers enjoy this challenge.

The leader uses jumping standards or two piles of books and places a light pole between the two posts. He adjusts the pole so that it will fall easily if brushed against by a player.

Couples or individuals line up, one behind the other, and take turns going under the bar. The object of the game is to see who can go under the bar when it is at the lowest point. If couples are in the contest together, they must hold hands while going under the bar. If either player disturbs the bar, causing it to fall, both players are eliminated. Start the contest with two people holding the bar at a height of about five feet. Lower the bar after all of the contestants have had an opportunity to go under it. When the bar is too low to walk or duck under, start using the pile of books for posts. Players may slide under the bar on their backs or crawl under on their stomachs. The bar is lowered until all but one couple or one individual have been eliminated. Award a prize to the winner.

NOTE TO THE LEADER

To make it easier to slide or crawl under the horizontal bar and to protect the clothing of the players, place a large piece of cardboard under the bar. Background music adds atmosphere and pleasure to this activity.

This is a good activity for a large "picnic group."

three blind mice

NUMBER OF PLAYERS—Eight up to any number, divided into four groups.

MATERIALS NEEDED—None.

Everyone knows this four-part singing round.

The leader divides the players into four groups. The players stand so that the four lines form a large square. All players stand facing the center of the square, and the leader gives each group a number: One, Two,

Three, Four. The players sing "Three Blind Mice" and at the same time go through the motions described below.

Players stand in line and face the center.

Three blind mice,	Three steps forward
Three blind mice–	Three steps backward

Each line faces to the right. Players place their hands on the shoulders of the person in front of them.

See how they run,	Three steps forward
See how they run!	Three steps backward

Players drop hands and each line faces the center again.

They all run after	Three steps forward
the farmer's wife.	Stop
She *cuts* (all clap)	Clap
off their tails with	Three steps backward
a carving knife.	Stop

Each line still facing the center.

Did you ever see such a sight in your life	Each person makes a complete turn in place to the right.
as three blind mice?	Stamp feet three times.

(Repeat three times)

After the players have gone through these motions and steps and are familiar with them, the leader instructs each group to start their singing and motions when he gives them the signal. Group one will begin. At the end of four measures the leader will signal group two to start. Group three and group four will begin when they receive the signal to start. This means each group will be singing different words and going in different directions. Each group stops after they have sung the song three times.

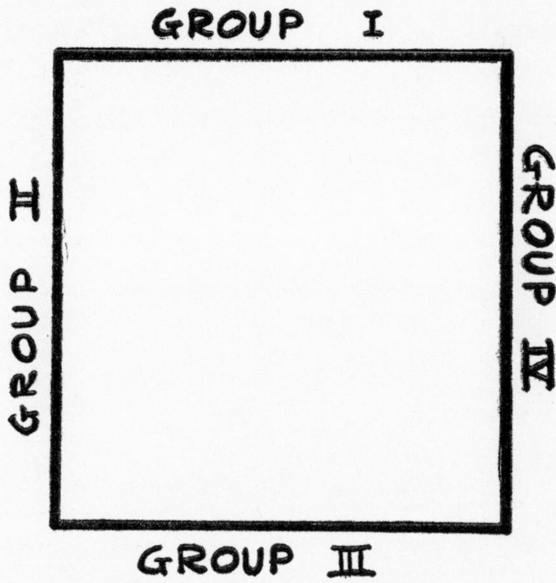

NOTE TO THE LEADER

Having the players line up in one straight line before you divide them into four groups makes it easier to familiarize them with the motions.

elimination dance

NUMBER OF PLAYERS—Any number, paired off in couples.
MATERIALS NEEDED—One paper swatter (or potato) for each couple.

To make swatters, roll four double sheets of newspaper together. Tape to keep them from unrolling.

This fun contest provides a lot of joy for the

teen-agers. The object for each couple is to try to stay in the dance as long as possible. The leader gives each couple a paper swatter (or potato) and explains what they are to do.

1. Partners face each other and place the swatter (or potato) flat against their foreheads. They hold the object in place by pressing against each other's foreheads.
2. When the music starts, the couples will dance or walk to the rhythm of the music, keeping the object in place between their foreheads.
3. Partners must keep both hands behind their backs.
4. When the swatter is dropped, the couple is *eliminated* and they leave the floor. (The swatter is returned to the leader.)

The last couple remaining on the dance floor are the winners and are awarded prizes.

NOTE TO THE LEADER

When there are only three or four couples left on the floor, announce that it is now permissible to *bump* other couples with the shoulders or hips in an effort to make the other couples drop their object.

over and under

NUMBER OF PLAYERS—Ten to a hundred couples.
MATERIALS NEEDED—Music.

This "warmer-upper" is easily taught, and teen-agers grasp the idea quickly. Whether there are ten or one hundred couples, in less than two minutes they are moving like old-timers and having fun.

Couples stand one behind the other forming a long line. The leader divides this line in *half* and instructs one column to face east and the other column to face west, so that the two columns of dancers are facing each other. Partners join inside hands. The first two couples start the over-and-under action by moving forward in the direction they are facing. The couple facing west raise their joined hands, and the couple facing east duck under these joined hands. Both couples continue moving forward alternately raising their hands *over* one couple's heads and going *under* the next couple's joined hands. The other couples start to move as soon as an approaching couple either ducks *under* their joined hands or passes joined hands *over* their heads. When couples reach the end of the line, they will *turn around* and continue going over and under each approaching couple's hands until they are back to their original place.

NOTE TO THE LEADER

Any sort of popular record can be used for this.

At both ends of the room establish a *turning point*. Mark the floor with chalk or place a chair at these points. Everyone must cross this line before turning around. Requiring couples to cross this line before reversing their direction keeps the group spread out and enables them to move without crowding.

patty cake polka

NUMBER OF PLAYERS—Any number, paired off in couples.
MATERIALS NEEDED—Polka record.

This is an ideal circle dance for teen-age groups. At the end of each chorus, each boy and each girl dance with a different partner.

Form a large double circle. Boys face the center of the circle. Girls stand facing their partners, with girls' backs to the center of the circle. Partners place both hands on each other's shoulders.

Actions	*How to Do It*
Heel! Toe! Heel! Toe!	With a slight hop, the boy touches his right heel to the floor in front, then touches his right toe to the floor behind and repeats this movement once more. The girl does the same, except she starts with her left heel.
Heel! Toe! Heel! Toe!	Both girl and boy repeat the step above.
Slide - Close - Slide Slide - Close - Slide Slide - Close - Slide	Both take three slide steps moving towards the boy's right.
Stamp! Stamp! Stamp!	Partners drop hands and stamp feet on the floor *three* times.
Right 1 - 2 - 3 (Clap Right Hands)	Both raise right hands shoulder-high and clap partner's hand *three* times.
Left 1 - 2 - 3 (Clap Left Hands)	Raise left hands and clap partner's left hand *three* times.
Both 1 - 2 - 3 (Clap Both Hands)	Raise both hands and clap both partner's hands *three* times.
Knees! 1 - 2 - 3 (Slap Own Knees)	Both bend forward and slap *own* knees three times.
Link Right Elbows and Swing.	Partners link right elbows and swing around *once*.

Boys move one person to the right, and everybody says "hello" to his new partner. Repeat the dance as often as desired.

shuffle

NUMBER OF PLAYERS—Ten to a hundred couples.
MATERIALS NEEDED—Music.

The SHUFFLE requires very little instruction, and teen-agers are delighted with the fun it affords.

Partners face each other and hold one another by both elbows, forming a long line. The leader divides the line in half. Couples in this position (holding elbows) weave forward and back around another couple. One column moves towards its *right;* the other column moves towards its *left.*

The first two couples nearest the center start the action. The couple on the left moves forward and around the first couple on their right. At the same time, the couple on the right moves backward around this same couple. Both couples continue moving alternately *forward* and *back*, weaving around each couple in line. The other couples start to move as soon as the approaching couple has passed either in front or in back of them. When couples reach the end of the line, they reverse the direction they are traveling and go back through the line in the opposite direction. They still continue to weave back and forth around each couple until they are back to their original place.

NOTE TO THE LEADER

Any sort of spirited record can be used to do the SHUFFLE.

At both ends of the room establish a *turning point.* Mark the floor with chalk or place a chair at these points. Requiring couples to cross this line before reversing their direction keeps the group spread out and enables them to move without crowding or bumping.

congo line

NUMBER OF PLAYERS—Any number. Eight to ten dancers in separate lines.

MATERIALS NEEDED—Music.

Forming Congo lines is always fun and a good way to break the ice at a party.

Eight to ten dancers stand one behind the other and place their hands on the waist of the person in front. There is no limit to the number of lines that can be formed.

The dancers start with the left foot and do the following steps: 1 - 2 - 3 steps forward and kick sideways with the right foot. Then starting with the right foot it's: 1 - 2 - 3 steps forward and kick sideways with the left foot. This is repeated while the leader of each line weaves in and out and goes in any direction on the floor. Any newcomers can hook onto the waist of the last person in any line and join the fun.

broomstick dance

NUMBER OF PLAYERS—Any number of couples plus one extra boy or girl.

MATERIALS NEEDED—A dressed up broomstick and music.

This is especially suitable for teen-age dancers who are inclined to dance with the same partner all evening.

All dancers except one are paired off with partners. Music is played, and the dancer without a partner must dance with the broom. When the music suddenly stops, the dancer with the broom drops it and grabs a partner. At the same time all other dancers must change partners. The person failing to get a partner must dance with the broom until the music stops again.

NOTE TO THE LEADER

Nail a cross-stick about shoulder-high to the broomstick. Dress the broom to look like a dancer–mop top and all. Everyone will want to dance with this beauty.

10 themes for special parties

Regardless of what we read and hear about teen-agers, ninety-nine per cent of them have high ideals and a keen sense of what is right and wrong. It is when "there is no place to go and nothing to do" that troubles crop up. Schools, homes, churches, and other worthwhile places need to open their doors to these young boys and girls and provide them with wholesome recreation, an opportunity to meet and learn to know each other in cheerful, healthful surroundings.

Parents and youth leaders play an important role in the lives of these young people. With the ingenuity, creativeness, vivaciousness, and imagination teen-agers possess, there is no limit to the number of good times that can be planned—providing the teen-agers have an understanding adult willing to help and direct them.

In this chapter we are suggesting themes for parties—to "spark" an idea for home, school, church, or other social get-togethers. For gatherings of the type described in this chapter, teen-agers are not usually invited to the party as couples. Informal get-togethers are much easier for unattached boys and girls. Both feel free to come even though they may not have started to date or may not be dating anyone at the time.

These informal affairs do not have to be elaborate or expensive to be a lot of fun. Supervision and guidance is of course necessary, but much of the planning and execution of the plans can be left to the teen-agers. Provide a place for the teen-agers to meet, give them whatever help they need, and let them prove their self-reliance.

great authors' party

Here's a way to plan a fun evening for a crowd. Tell the group not to come to the party in costumes, but to dress to represent the title of any book on the suggested reading list in English. For instance, a boy with a horn would depict Dorothy Baker's *Young Man with a Horn*, or a girl wearing a red badge would symbolize Stephen Crane's *Red Badge of Courage*. Others might represent *Look to the Mountains*, *Keys to the Kingdom*, *Drums Along the Mohawk*, *Laughing Boy*, or *Young Bess*. The fellows and girls try to guess the titles of the book each person's clothing represents.

Tell them not to give away their guesses; but to be sure they don't, here's a good speech-squelcher and also a smile-provoker. As soon as the contest starts, hand every individual a piece of cardboard to place between his or her teeth. The pasteboard must not be removed until the call "Time's up."

Give each person a pencil and a piece of paper and tell him to write the names of the persons wearing the costumes, the title of the book each represents, and the author of the book. When ample time has been allowed for this, the guests sit down and go over their lists to determine who guessed the most titles and authors. Anyone whose depiction mystified everyone must prove himself.

taffy pulling party

This taffy pulling party is a dandy, because while making the taffy the boys often get stuck to the girls. Did you ever hear the expression "He's stuck on her?" Well, this is where it started! If your crowd has never had a taffy pull, give them a big treat and plan one.

When the fellows and girls arrive, they go straight to the kitchen. Have some big, buttered platters ready. Spread waxed paper over a clean table top. Now they are ready to start the big mix. Into an extra-large saucepan, put two cups of molasses, a pinch of salt, a lump of butter, and a thermometer. Turn the heat on low. Guests take turns stirring the mixture faithfully until the thermometer registers 254°. (No thermometer? Then stir until syrup is hard, almost brittle, when dropped into a cup of cold water.) When done, pour the mixture into the buttered platters. Let it cool. This takes time, so plan some games or dancing until the taffy is ready to pull. Now comes the fun.

First, get ready for the pulling. Hands should be washed thoroughly, then buttered (the butter keeps the taffy from sticking). It's fun for a fellow and his girl to work together. Each couple gathers up as much taffy as they can handle. Then they start pulling and stretching. The candy gets lighter and lighter, shinier and shinier, and stickier and stickier. When someone shouts, "It's getting tough to pull," it's time now for the boy and his partner to put their batches together and unite forces. Keep buttering hands if the taffy is sticking. When the taffy starts to get brittle, or the piece someone is sampling makes a clicking sound when he taps it against his front teeth, it's time to stop pulling. Stretch the candy out like a long rope and twist it into a pretty design, then curl it out on the wax paper. Cut it into chunks. Everyone had fun—and probably liked the taffy too.

tune detective

Everyone who plays a musical instrument brings it to the party. Each fellow and girl brings two or three favorite records, each marked with a name so that there won't be any mix-ups.

Collect the records. Start playing a record at the beginning, middle, or anywhere and play it for just a couple of seconds. Who can name the tune first? On with another record. Who recognizes it first? To make a real game out of TUNE DETECTIVE, divide the group into teams or play as couples. Give each group a pencil and a piece of paper to write the titles. Give a prize to the group who recognizes the most tunes.

band concert

Have a band concert. Give each person an instrument to play, such as a kazoo that carries the melody when the player hums through them, combs covered with tissue paper, tin plates, pan lids, pieces of wood cut from a broomstick, tin cans filled with popcorn or dried beans, blocks of wood covered with sand paper, or anything else that will make sound. Choose a leader, and have the band play on.

halloween party

If the bunch wants to have a Halloween party that is not too silly, a little more on the sophisticated side, try this.

Ask them to come wearing a hat they have styled from goodness-knows-what to represent the Spirit of Halloween—witch, cat, bat, owl, graveyard, skeletons, devils, pumpkins, or any thing else they can think of. The rest of the costume—just their regular Saturday night outfits.

Have several besheeted ghosts ready to meet the fellows and girls at the door, one with a weak, shaky "Hello, come in." A second ghost extends a cold, clammy hand—a rubber glove filled with wet sand and refrigerated for the last hour. The third ghost escorts the guest through the Chamber of Horror. Old fur coats are hung so they will be brushed against. Many long strings of thread hung from the top of a doorway will feel like cobwebs. Of course, have a ghost rattling chains and giving out horrible moans somewhere along the path.

Keep the lights dim and use some Halloween decorations such as pumpkins, husky ears of corn, apples, gourds, and the like. Make enormous black paper cats and outline them with luminous paint or tape. Then work out special ghostly ideas like the following.

THE MURDER OF HERBERT SMEAR

Try this for a shrieking success. Everyone is seated in a circle. Dim the lights. A record player on slow speed makes spooky music, and a talking or singing record produces weird sounds. Play such a record, very softy, for a ghostly background effect.

The leader enters the room draped in a sheet,

with a flashlight concealed beneath the sheet in such a way as to throw a light upon his face. He reads the following poem, using an ominous voice, pausing at specific times while his assistants pass the articles mentioned.

The Murder of Herbert Smear

Listen, my children, and you shall hear
About a murder which happened here
Upon a night both dark and drear
To a poor old man called Herbert Smear.

I have with me the man's remains.
Of them, I pass you now his brains!
(Pass a moist sponge)

His eyes were blue; his skin was fair;
And soft and silky was his hair.
(Pass pieces of fur or corn silk)

An old man, he could barely hear.
Caress poor Herbert's deaf old ear.
(Pass dried peaches or apricots)

As the murderer struck the blow unheard,
This windpipe forced out Smear's last word!
(Pass lengths of uncut, cold, boiled macaroni)

The ghastly grin of death did wreath
This set of gleaming, pearly teeth.
(Pass kernels of dried corn)

Slowly, Smear's poor corpse grew cold.
I give you now his hand to hold.
(Pass rubber glove stuffed with cold, wet sand)

If only Smear had been more wise
His head might still contain these eyes.
(Pass peeled grapes)

Although they're dry and brittle now,
Smear's backbone once made courtly bows.
(Pass empty spools strung on cord)

This sound should melt a heart of stone
The mournful rattle of Smear's old bones!
(Chains rattle)

By Doris Snell

NOTE TO THE LEADER

End this gruesome stunt by giving a loud scream, and everyone in the circle will scream. Don't use this stunt with very young children. It will frighten them too much.

A WEIGHTY PROBLEM SOLVED

Characters:
Mrs. Thin
Mrs. Stout
Witch Doctor

The costume for the Witch Doctor is a long cape, an ugly mask, a witch hat, and a satchel.

Two large umbrellas, two balloons, and two sheets are used for the costumes of Mrs. Thin and Mrs. Stout. Blow balloons up and tie one to the tip of each umbrella. Paint faces on the balloons and place a Halloween party hat on each. Wrap a sheet around the top of each umbrella. Mrs. Thin envelopes herself in the sheet, holds up her umbrella unopened, and Mrs. Stout does likewise except that her umbrella is opened.

The balloon-faced ladies enter. Mrs. Thin and Mrs. Stout discuss the popular subject of weight, each wishing to be the reverse. Along comes the Witch Doctor. After much examining and diagnosing, he hands Mrs. Thin a yeast cake and Mrs. Stout an eighteen-day diet book. Immediately, Mrs. Thin opens her umbrella and Mrs. Stout closes hers. Now everyone's happy.

APPLE FATE (a fortunetelling stunt)

Halloween just wouldn't be Halloween without one fortunetelling stunt for those who want to know the initials of their future lifetime mate. Each should peel an apple in as long and thin a spiral as he can, then toss the peeling over his left shoulder. It will form the initial of his future spouse.

everybody up and doing party

Try this some evening. It's fun for everyone.

When planning the party, sit down and make a list of all the necessary little things that will have to be done during the evening. Prepare tags with these duties written on them. As each guest arrives, he draws a tag from a hat. He writes his name under the message on the tag and pins the tag on clothing near his shoulder. He will know, and so will the rest of the fellows and girls, what his job is for the evening. Here are some suggestions for the tags:

I'm the official greeter.
I'll hang up your wraps.
I'm serving dessert.
I'll get you a bottle of pop.
Someone you don't know?
I'll introduce you.

I'm staying to help tidy up.
Need potato chips? Ask me.
Call me if anything spills.
I'm clearing the dishes.
Lucky me.
I'm not doing anything.

It won't take long for everyone to get into action and keep his friends stepping, perhaps unnecessarily, but it all adds to the fun. Asking those attending the party to add their support always makes a party more interesting and exciting.

hobo party

Teen-agers get a bang out of this kind of get-together. It makes a nice home party.

The fellows and girls come to the party dressed as hobos. Each brings a coffee can containing a cut-up or diced vegetable of his own choice. The only preparation for the hostess is a large kettle of partially cooked stewing meat and a large spoon for stirring. As each person arrives, he goes immediately to the kitchen, adds his vegetable to the stew, and gives it a stir. Then he rinses the can so that it will be ready for use later on. The stew cooks while the guests dance or play a few games. When it is time to serve, the guests line up in cafeteria style and, carrying the coffee can they brought, help themselves to some stew. This is oodles of fun and can easily be turned into a patio or back yard party.

scavenger hunt

What could be more fun than blue jeans, a campfire, hot dogs, good friends together, and a scavenger hunt?

Here's what to do. Invite the bunch, tell them to wear blue jeans, and ask each girl to bring four franks. The hostess can furnish the buns, pop, relish, and cookies. Have the get-together in a back yard or picnic area and use balloons to give it all a festive look.

Divide up the fellows and girls or have them draw numbers so that they can hunt in groups of four or six. Give each group a list of the things they are to collect and bring back as soon as possible. Remind them that they are to *stay together*. It's not fair to be scattering in all directions to find the items. On the signal "Go," each group starts to hunt.

Here are some suggestions for the scavenger hunt list: Empty soup can, a baby rattle, bottle top, first page of last Sunday's newspaper, last year's calendar, pencil with red lead, an artificial flower, toy pistol—and just anything you can think of. Reward the first team to return with all the articles mentioned on their list.

Sing songs, ask riddles, repeat tongue twisters, have lots to eat and lots of fun.

NOTE TO THE LEADER

Never put anything on a scavenger hunt list that will get the group in trouble or be a nuisance to others. Make up the list carefully.

mad hatter party

A MAD HATTER PARTY is fun and, believe it or not, the boys get a big charge out of one of these parties. This is a lively idea for a small group, or it can be used for big affairs. It makes a good Spring party.

At a MAD HATTER PARTY, everyone wears a crazy, wild, mad, goofy, nutty, fantastic hat of his own creation. Some of the guests might decide to wear a wooden salad bowl filled with beautifully arranged vegetables, or a bird's nest with a mother hen sitting on eggs. They'll have some crazy ideas. Be sure to have a fashion parade and appoint a couple of fellows to act as judges. Have them pick out the cleverest, funniest, prettiest, most fantastic, and most elaborate hat and give every winner a silly prize.

Taking pictures of groups, solos, or couples adds a lot to the fun and will be a big laugh all over again when reviewed later.

Plan some dancing and play a few of the gang's favorite games.

hawaiian party

Greet the group by placing a lei around each one's neck. Provide newspaper or crepe paper, scissors, etc., and have each guest make a grass skirt for himself to wear the rest of the evening.

Split a watermelon in half, fill it with ginger ale, and place it on a table. Add ice cubes to keep it cool. If anyone gets thirsty, he helps himself to a straw and drinks to his heart's desire. It's fun if two or three fellows and girls drink at the same time.

Have some Hawaiian music going on the record player and get one of the girls to lead the group in a Hawaiian dance. Doing the Limbo (Chapter 9) will limber up the gang, and they'll all have a back-bending good time.

gypsy picnic

For an outdoor gathering it would be ideal if a horse and wagon and a back country road could be found. The horse and wagon could be decorated with flowers and streamers. If such goings-on are impossible, someone's Dad might just love to take the gang in his truck, all decorated for the occasion. Or go on foot like raggle-taggle gypsies, wearing gaudy bangles, kerchiefs, and sashes, the boys in cut-off dungarees and wearing one earring.

At the picnic area, the gypsy men can start a fire under a big kettle for soup, stew, or chowder. While the stew simmers, plan some gypsy activities like fortune-telling, horseshoe pitching, circle games, and fast dancing. If anyone in the crowd plays a guitar, accordion, harmonica, or any other suitable instrument, be sure to have a sing-song as the evening sun goes down.

coney island picnic

The group can have real fun at this kind of an affair. It takes some work to prepare, but that's half the fun. With everyone pitching in, it's amazing what can be done in not too long a time.

A patio, tennis court, or other outdoor area becomes the Midway. On it line up a few tables for the different carnival games. Give the tables a gala look with wild-colored crepe-paper skirts. Umbrellas can be bedecked with balloons to add to the festive look.

Tell everyone to come dressed in street fair get-up—make up, black moustaches, and all. Issue paper money. Barkers and vendors can cry in true carnival voices: "Right this way, folks, step right up and try your luck, you might be the lucky winner!"

SUGGESTIONS FOR AMUSEMENT STAND:

Mark three coffee cans with different values. Try to bounce three balls into the cans. Try for high score.

Tack inflated balloons to heavy cardboard and use three darts to attempt to break the balloons. Five points for every broken balloon. Prizes.

Paste numbers from an old calendar in different compartments of a muffin tin. Toss three ping-pong balls. Try for high score.

Drive nails partway into a piece of plywood and mark their value. Toss five jar rings. Try for high score.

Set up plastic bowling pins as in bowling. Roll two balls to knock them all over. (Look around and collect other gadgets you could use.)

Grab Bag. Fill a large dishpan half full of sawdust (any lumber dealer will give you all you need). Put pennies, paper-wrapped candy, small trinkets, chewing gum, etc., into the sawdust and mix it around. The fellows and girls can use only one hand and and have only three chances to find something. Sand can be substituted for sawdust.

an old-fashioned party

This kind of party can be a riot. The guests wear old-fashioned attire and bring pictures of themselves taken way back when they were very young.

As the group arrives, the pictures are placed on a table with a number identifying each one. Later on, after the fellows and girls have enjoyed some dancing, give each person a pencil and paper to write the name of the person in pictures 1, 2, 3, etc. Some of the guests can't believe their eyes.

st. patrick's day party

St. Patrick's Day parties can be oodles of fun. The guys and gals come wearing as much green as they can. As they arrive, give each person a paper apron or tie. It's amazing how putting on something silly, like aprons or hats, will put people in a gay party spirit.

Have a record player and lots of dance records on hand. Try to locate an Irish jig. Get as many records of famous Irish melodies as you can and use them for background music throughout the evening.

As the gang dribbles in, first-comers can dance or talk. Later maybe some of the group can give out with real barbershop harmony and sing Irish songs: "My

Wild Irish Rose," "Mother Machree," "When Irish Eyes Are Smiling," and others.

Get one of the fellows or girls who knows something about art to draw a large picture of an Irishman's face and place it on the wall. Play "Put the Pipe in O'Leary's Mouth," just like the old game of Pin the Tail on the Donkey.

Green punch and green cupcakes will add an Irish touch.

costume party themes

Here are a few more types of dress-up parties your group might enjoy. Dress-up parties give everyone a chance to be as original, humorous, clever, pretty, and as funny or sedate as he cares to be.

COMIC STRIP CHARACTERS

The fellows and girls come to the party dressed as comic strip characters. Provide each person with a pencil and paper and award a prize to the one who can identify the most characters.

COME-AS-YOU-ARE-NOW PARTY

Call the group on the phone. Tell them the date of the party and explain to them that they are to come to the party dressed "as you are now."

WRONG WAY, BACKWARD, UPSIDE DOWN, INSIDE OUT PARTY

At this party everything possible is done the wrong way around. The guests are welcomed at the back door with a cordial "goodbye." Costumes are worn wrong side out, inside out, or even upside down. Crazy costumes and crazy touches around the room, pictures upside down, and furniture at different angles all add to the fun.

little sister party

A group of teen-agers could have a lot of fun planning an afternoon party for little sisters and the smaller children in the neighborhood. Play games, run races, and feature a baby carriage parade. Have each little girl, with one of the teen-ager's help, dress her doll and decorate the carriage. Have a parade and give a prize to the best "mother and child."

how does your boyfriend rate?

(for all-girl group)

Girls always talk about their boyfriends when they are together, so here's a way to find out if he is an all-around boy with a solid character and one who would be a pretty safe bet for marriage or if he is a boy who has need for improvement in some ways.

Using thin sheets of paper, the hostess traces the picture found on this page. She should make one or two pictures for each guest.

When the girls are ready to rate their boy friends, give each girl a pencil and a picture. Here is how the game is played: Every girl thinks of a boy she likes. The hostess slowly reads the questions that follow, and each girl rates the boy she is thinking of. Of course, to get a correct picture, the girls will have to use their judgment and give honest answers. Each time the answer to the question is "yes," the girl draws a straight line to the next dot. If her picture is complete, her "dream boy" measures up to be a "real guy."

1
21
2
20
5
17

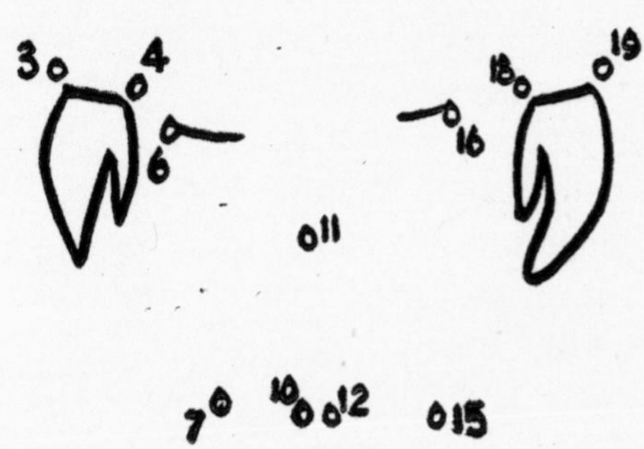
3
4
18
19
6
16
11
7
10
12
15

8
9
13
14

QUESTIONS FOR YOUNG TEENS

1. Does he come to school looking neat and clean?
2. Do almost all the boys and girls like him?
3. Does he get along well with his teachers?
4. Is he almost always pleasant and cheerful?
5. Does he have a paper route or any other paying job?
6. Does he belong to the Boy Scouts, YMCA, a church group, or any other worthwhile organization?
7. Does he have any hobbies?
8. Is he polite to you and older people?
9. Do you like the things he says and the way he talks?
10. Are you really proud to be seen with him?
11. Does he talk about interesting things?
12. Does he always keep his promises?
13. Does he treat you with respect?
14. Does he attend religious services regularly?
15. Do your mother and father like him?
16. Does he make average or better than average grades?
17. Is he interested in sports?
18. Is he almost always on time for appointments?
19. Does he honor your wishes and the wishes of your parents even if they are not to his liking?
20. Is he always thoughtful of the other person?
21. Does he say words such as "Please, Thank you," and "I'm sorry" when they are called for?

QUESTIONS FOR OLDER TEENS

1. Does he dress neatly and modestly without a tendency toward gaudiness or overdressing?
2. Does he enjoy doing little pleasant things for you?

3. Is he friendly and sincerely interested in other people?
4. Is he interested in world happenings, politics, business, or any other worthwhile subjects?
5. Can he forgive past mistakes without dwelling on them?
6. Is he loyal to his friends, minimizing or not mentioning their faults to others?
7. Is he free from "touchiness," so that others don't have to handle him with kid gloves?
8. Does he act according to his honest convictions, and is he able to say "no," regardless of what the rest of the fellows might think?
9. Does he use good English and refrain from the use of excess slang, profanity, or vulgarity?
10. Can you depend upon him to do what he says he will do when he says he will do it?
11. Is he usually on good terms with his family and friends?
12. Does he enter into informal social events of many types wholeheartedly?
13. If he drives a car, does he obey all traffic rules and regulations?
14. Is he making definite plans and preparations for his future?
15. Does he frequently put you first? Is he concerned about your interests as well as his own?
16. If a difference of opinion comes up, can you work it out together by mutual understanding?
17. Does he have a goal he wishes to reach and is eager

to accomplish and achieve?

18. Can you converse easily with him and feel that you want to share many thoughts and interests with him?
19. When you make plans does he say: "What we shall do, what we shall enjoy, what we shall like," instead of saying "I"?
20. Like and love are two different words. Do you *like* 99 per cent of everything about him?
21. Has your love continued through trouble and trials (anger, resentment, fear, sorrow) as well as through joys?

If you completed the picture with honest answers, the chances are that you two could have a lifetime of happiness. Beware if your picture is not complete. You are substituting false emotions for love.

Index